# Teacher Education and the Cultural Imagination

## Autobiography, Conversation, and Narrative

# Teacher Education and the Cultural Imagination

## *Autobiography, Conversation, and Narrative*

ॐ

### *Susan Florio-Ruane*

**Michigan State University**

***With the assistance of Julie deTar***

**LEA**

2001

LAWRENCE ERLBAUM ASSOCIATES, PUBLISHERS
Mahwah, New Jersey                                         London

The author thanks Helen Barolini for permission to quote from her edited volume, *The Dream Book: An Anthology of Writings by Italian American Women,* originally published by Schocken Books in 1985. A revised of this book is published by Syracuse University Press (2000).

Portions of this text were adapted from material previously published by the authors in the following articles: Florio-Ruane, S. and deTar, J. (1995). Conflict and consensus in teacher candidates' discussion of ethnic autobiography. *English Education,* vol. 27, no. 1, pp. 11–39, and Florio-Ruane, S. (1997). CAE 1996 Presidential address—To tell a new story: Reinventing narratives of culture, identity, and education. *Anthropology and Education Quarterly.* Vol. 28, no. 2, pp. 152–162.

Lawrence Erlbaum Associates, Inc., Publishers
10 Industrial Avenue
Mahwah, NJ 07430

Cover design by Kathryn Houghtaling Lacey

**Library of Congress Cataloging-in-Publication Data**
Florio-Ruane, Susan.
  Teacher education and cultural imagination: autobiography, conversation, and narrative
/ by Susan Florio-Ruane with the assistance of Julie de Tar.
    p.   cm.
  Includes bibliographical references (p.) and index.
  ISBN 0-8058-2374-3 (cloth: alk. paper)—ISBN 0-8058-2375-1 (pbk.: alk. paper)
    1. Education—United States—Bibliographical methods. 2. Teachers—Training of—United
States. 3. Multicultural education—United States. 4. Group reading—United States. I.
DeTar, Julie. II. Title.

LB1029.B55 F56 2000
370'.092'2—dc21                                                                    00-062253

Printed in the United States of America
10  9  8  7  6  5  4  3  2  1

To the memory of my mother, Rita,
and for my niece, Samantha,
who is learning to keep the family stories
and tell new ones of her own.

*"She is part of me now, total and consoling. And it is not a sadness to acknowledge that she had to die before I could know her fully. It is only a statement of the power of what comes after."*
—Don DeLillo, *Underworld* (1997, p. 804)

# Contents

# List of Figures
# and Tables

**FIGURES**

## TABLES

# Foreword

The 29 preservice teachers sit in a large circle, listening attentively as my colleague Margie Maaka begins the activity she calls cultural sharing. Margie has instructed the preservice teachers to bring three objects that represent their cultural backgrounds. Taking her turn first, she presents a kaleidoscope made of kauri, a wood from her New Zealand homeland. Margie compares the kaleidoscope, with its blend of Polynesian and western elements, to her own Maori and Pakeha (British/Dutch) ethnicity. The preservice teachers display a range of objects that include an 'uli'uli (a gourd rattle used in the hula), family photos, a soccer ball, grunge clothing, postcards of Impressionist paintings, a candle, and an American flag. Three students have brought Hawaiian–English dictionaries as symbols of their interest in the Hawaiian language. When my turn comes, I show the group a t-shirt from a recent reunion of my father's family and speak about my great-grandfather, a Chinese immigrant who ran a rice mill and plantation on the island of Kaua'i.

This scene took place on the campus of an elementary school on the Leeward Coast of O'ahu, a low-income area in which about two-thirds of the students are of Native Hawaiian ancestry. Margie and I conduct the Ka Lama teacher education initiative to prepare teachers to teach in Leeward Coast elementary schools. We have tried to recruit residents of the community to become teachers, and the ethnic make-up of our cohorts of preservice teachers do not resemble those anywhere else. Over one-third of the preservice teachers are Native Hawaiians, with the next largest groups being Filipino and Japanese Americans.

As you can tell, issues of culture, diversity, and equity are at the heart of my work as a teacher educator. I read Susan's manuscript with great interest because of its focus on these very issues. Susan argues for the importance of addressing the role of culture in our own lives, as teachers and teacher educators, as a way of gaining insights about the role of culture in the lives of our students. Few steps can be more vital to improving education for the many students of diverse cultural and linguistic backgrounds who already constitute the majority in every urban school district in the United States.

This fall, Margie and I are beginning to see the effects of our efforts to increase the number of Native Hawaiian teachers on the Leeward Coast. In the classrooms of Ka Lama graduates, students of diverse backgrounds are being taught by teachers who share their cultural heritage. But I know how unusual our situation is. In the contiguous states, while the student population has grown increasingly diverse, the proportion of teachers of diverse backgrounds has continued to shrink.

Common in inner city schools, and likely to be common for the foreseeable future, are classrooms in which students of diverse backgrounds are taught by Euro American teachers who grew up in suburbs or small towns. These classrooms become contact zones in which teachers and students must cross cultural boundaries to negotiate relationships. In the best cases, teachers and students creatively construct hybrid cultures, unlike those found in the home or typical classroom, in which communication and learning flourish. In the worst cases, teachers and students find themselves locked in a year-long stand-off in which neither side can afford to yield ground. One of our goals must be to prepare teachers of mainstream backgrounds to engage students of diverse backgrounds in the process of constructing hybrid classroom cultures, in which students can reach high levels of academic achievement while maintaining their cultural identities.

A past president of the Council on Anthropology and Education, Susan has been a leader in the movement to bring anthropological theory and method to bear on the knotty issues of American education. While earlier generations of anthropologists journeyed afar to "make the strange familiar," Susan and her colleagues have stayed at home, seeking to "make the familiar strange."

In the research presented here, Susan took on the challenge of guiding Euro American teachers to explore issues of culture and to see themselves as cultural beings.

I was reminded of my first day in a graduate course on educational anthropology. The professor asked us to write down the term we would use to describe our ethnicity. She picked up my paper, on which I had written Chinese American, and contrasted it to the response of the student sitting next to me, who had simply written American. This student insisted that was all he could write, because he had never seen himself as anything but just plain American. Susan makes the point that those who are outside the mainstream are more likely to recognize the difference between the marked and unmarked form. Those within the mainstream, the unmarked form, are often less able to recognize themselves as such. Because the teachers in her work were all of mainstream backgrounds, Susan found that her task could be compared to helping fish become aware of the water surrounding them.

Susan hypothesized that the reading and discussion of autobiographies might help the teachers to better understand their own culture, as well as to gain insights about other cultures. The works read included Maya Angelou's classic, *I Know Why the Caged Bird Sings*. As Susan hoped, the teachers often found that what began as a window into the life of another turned into a mirror upon their own lives.

Changes in the teachers' understandings of culture took place in the twists and turns of conversations among small groups of colleagues. At the heart of Susan's work was a constructivist, conversational approach to teaching and learning centered on literature discussion circles or Book Clubs. When Susan guided the teachers' discussions of the autobiographies, she was an active participant, more than an observer or even a participant observer. As a participant, she had to come to terms with her own thinking about issues of culture. One of the themes in this volume is that we as teacher educators must undertake our own cultural journeys, if we are to engage the teachers with whom we work in similar explorations.

What emboldens teachers to embark upon and continue these journeys is membership in a community of learners. When disagreements arose, participants in the Book Clubs took pains to express their views in a manner that did not damage their relationships to others or jeopardize the community. Within an atmosphere of trust, members felt they could speak openly and honestly about such troubling topics as racism and inequality. Susan's analyses show that some teachers persisted in nudging others to think more deeply about issues, thus furthering understanding within the group. Membership in such learning communities is essential because, as Susan found, the task of arriving at shared insights about culture was both intellectually and emotionally demanding, a matter not of a few weeks but of two years or more.

As a narrative about narratives, this book is bounded at beginning and end by Susan's reflections on her personal experiences as a teacher educator and Italian American. In the beginning and ending chapters, in particular, Susan demonstrates the the power of research and reflection about culture by using the example of her own life. The power of constructivist approaches is just this—that the teacher must be a living example of the approaches and values being espoused. As teachers, we must find the courage to know ourselves as cultural beings, to recognize that we— teachers and students alike—are all more than just plain Americans.

Kathryn Au
Honolulu, Hawaii

# Acknowledgments

In a letter to his editor, John Steinbeck (1969) wrote, "A book is like a man—clever and dull, brave and cowardly, beautiful and ugly. For every flowering thought there will be a page like a wet and mangy mongrel" (p. 238). I thank the following people for providing the support I needed to create the occasional flowering thought. The wet and mangy mongrels are my sole responsibility.

I am grateful to Julie deTar for her friendship and contributions as both participant and research colleague in the Future Teachers' Autobiography Club. Her insistent, thoughtful questions kept me focused on what matters to teachers and their learning. I also thank Virginia Goatley for her advice as I adapted children's book clubs to teacher education. Patricia Stock, whose work on dialogic curriculum was important in my learning, published fledgling reports of this project in *English Education*. At Lawrence Erlbaum Associates, Publishers, Naomi Silverman was a patient editor and a smart, caring colleague.

I received funding for this work from several sources. Penelope Peterson helped me initiate research on the Future Teachers' Autobiography Club with a seed grant from the Michigan State University College of Education. My research collaboration with Julie deTar was supported by a small grant from the Spencer Foundation, where Catherine Lacey was an insightful reader and respondent. A study of teacher learning in the course, "Culture, Literacy, and Autobiography" was funded by a grant-in-aide awarded to Taffy Raphael and myself from the National Council of Teachers of English. My analysis of the Literary Circle in the final stages of writing this book was supported by the National Center for Improvement of Early Reading Achievement under the direction of P. David Pearson.[1]

In the early 1990s, Taffy Raphael conducted innovative studies of children's learning in book clubs. I was fortunate to join a local public library Book Talk Group with Taffy and her research assistant, Virginia Goatley, in 1992. That experience opened my eyes to the potential of book clubs for adult learning. As it happened, the librarian who led the group had a special interest in immigrant autobiography and fiction. Thus, I was introduced to the power of the literary imagination to bring the cultural experience to life. The following year, I created the Future Teachers' Autobiography Club. Subsequently, I designed and taught a course for experienced literacy teachers on "Culture, Literacy, and Autobiography." With Taffy and doctoral students, Mary McVee, Susan Wallace-Cowell, Jocelyn Glazier, and Bette Shellhorn, I researched teachers' learning in that course and in a book club that class members formed after the course ended. I owe a substantial intellectual debt to this bright, companionable group of colleagues.

My friends and family took an interest in this work and kept me at it with good-natured prodding. I wish to thank especially Jeffrey Shultz, Janet Theophano, Christopher Clark, Katie Anderson-Levitt, Paula Salvio, Mike Rose, Jenny Denyer, Catherine Lacey, Karen Eisele, Patrick Ruane, Karla Bellingar, Nina Hasty, June Haas, Jennifer Berne, Patricia Edwards, James Gavelek, Elizabeth deRath, Ebony Roberts, Suzanne Wilson, Claire Simon, Vincent Florio, and Maggie Lampert. Several others inspired this work and remained at its heart throughout. To say that Taffy Raphael has been my colleague and friend does not begin to capture what I have learned from her generous intelligence and ample good humor. And my father, Frank Florio, who died just as this book was completed, understood this work as a labor of love and sustained my effort with a bounty of family stories and memories. My husband, Tom Ruane,

[1]The research described in this volume was supported in part by the Educational Research and Development Centers Program, PR/Award Number R305R70004, administered by the Office of Educational Research and Improvement, U.S. Department of Education. The contents of the report do not necessarily represent the position, policies or endorsement of the National Institute on Student Achievement, Curriculum, and Assessment or the National Institute on Early Childhood Development, the U.S. Department of Education, or the federal government.

urged me to think hard about my topic but also to remember that serious work is best accomplished with a light, loving touch. Finally, the members of the Future Teachers' Autobiography Club and the Literary Circle gave life to this project. Although a promise of privacy precludes naming them here, one could not wish for better company, and I thank them all.

# Introduction

Seated cross-legged on my living room carpet, I am hosting the first meeting of the Future Teachers' Autobiography Club. The six young women gathered with me around the coffee table are student teachers. The members of this newly formed club are classmates in "The Learning Community," a teacher education program I helped design. Like most undergraduate teacher candidates at my university, these young women come from rural and suburban backgrounds. Some consider themselves fortunate to be teaching in schools and communities similar to those where they grew up. A few who have been placed for student teaching in the nearby state capital are working with economically and culturally diverse youngsters. Despite the December chill, they arrive at my door flushed with the excitement of solo teaching. Although they will have very busy lives during the next 6 months, each accepted my invitation to gather monthly for dinner and book talk. Certainly the food and the chance to reconnect with classmates draw them to the club. But they are also drawn by the topic. I have invited them to read and discuss six books. These books are enticing because they are life stories and also because they are stories of culture.

In preparation for our first meeting, we have read Vivian Paley's (1979/1989) book, *White Teacher*. Some of us have read excerpts before, but reading the entire book and talking with others about it over dinner is a novel experience. Everyone arrives with a paperback copy in hand. Some have scribbled notes in the margins. Others have folded down corners of pages containing memorable passages. As we settle down to the meal, the young women work to balance being both dinner guest and book discussant. *White Teacher* is a coming of age memoir. In it, Paley describes her novice teaching in a Chicago preschool. Like many of us, she is a cultural "pastiche." Middle class, Jewish, female, and from the South, she arrives in Chicago unaccustomed to teaching, confronted with her first African-American pupils, and raised to believe that avoiding mention of race is a way of showing tolerance and politeness.

Teachers' stories like Paley's have been praised for their imaginative crafting of the "messy voice of practice" in literature (Ballenger, 1999, p. 10). But these personal teaching narratives have also been critiqued for their tendency to isolate the teacher as both source of and solution to the problems of her practice (Cazden, cited in Ballenger, 1999, pp. vii–viii). The genre is oddly both compelling and inert—telling readers about the complexity of "real teaching," but in singular, heroic voices. If teachers are, indeed, "lone rangers," then they must be heroes if they are to solve the problems of their practice. The stories can make us feel intimidated and lonely. What can we learn from autobiographies? How might they help us imagine our own lives and teaching practice in new and perhaps more powerful ways? One way teachers can learn from personal narratives is by reading them in the company of colleagues. As members of an autobiography book club, we are taking two typically solitary activities—reading books and thinking about problems in our own practice—and making of them conversational common ground. Moreover, we are taking a genre typically thought of as personal and individual and reading it as a dialogic one.

Deceptively easy to read, the anecdotes making up Paley's book lure us into risky, self-searching places. Talk about culture and race does not come easily for Paley. And, even in my cozy living room, it does not come easily for us. As we begin our meal, buttering bread and passing serving plates, we talk about Paley's gradual insight into her own cultural background and her assumptions about others. We visit her discovery of the limits and consequences of the colorblindness she adopted when dealing with African-American pupils. To this point, we have been polite dinner

## Nell's Story

Once upon a time, a little girl named Nell was assigned to prepare an oral report about her cultural background. Nell realized that she did not know very much about hers. What could she say that would give her report the flavor and color of "culture"? Nell felt a wave of panic as she thought about what to show and tell. "I'm not anything," she thought, "I'm just an American." Seeking to impress her teacher and classmates with at least some colorful details of her family's food, dress, and holidays, Nell asked her mother for help. But Nell was disappointed when, barely looking up from the vegetables she was preparing for dinner, her mother merely shrugged at the question, "What are we?" She replied, "I don't know. Some mix of Irish and English, I guess. It was along time ago." When pressed, her mother could summon none of the colorful details Nell hoped to include in her report. Frustrated and desperate for a story, Nell tells us, "I dreaded having to give that report." So, she confesses, to make her cultural background interesting, "I faked being from Poland."

companions, and Paley's story has been essentially what my colleague Taffy Raphael calls a "museum piece." We circle the text, noticing its lines and shapes, but not touching its theme. Yet, perhaps warmed by the satisfying meal and Paley's engaging prose, we gradually begin to talk in ways that feel less like a seminar or formal dinner, and more like a conversation among friends. As we do this, we begin to engage with Paley's theme in terms of our own lives, in the here and now of our teaching and in memories of childhood.

Like Paley, those of us at the table are "White teachers" and like her we have much to learn not only about the diverse youngsters we teach, but also about ourselves. To learn about "others" we need to look both outward and inward. We do not initially take up Paley's gambit by addressing race, a theme we will approach gingerly over multiple dinners and books. But we do begin to talk about Paley's narrative in terms of our own formation and how culture arises in our work as educators. In this act of imagination and memory we come closer the idea of culture by telling stories. As plates are cleared and dessert is served, our laughter increases, and our rising voices begin to overlap. We seem to be scrambling to get hold of the topic of culture in our own remembered lives. Nell's[1] voice is the first to emerge. Well liked by her peers, she speaks easily and often. So it is not surprising that other voices quiet as Nell begins the story of a multicultural festival in which she participated as a child. Almost as if she had started with, "Once upon a time," we settle into story-listening, awaiting Nell's problem, its complicating action, and its ultimate resolution.

I have retold Nell's story because I think it embodies the problem of culture's elusiveness in the education of both teachers and children in our society. Although its resolution serves the youngster's immediate need for a compelling story, how has Nell's experience shaped her consciousness as an educator? Read one way, it illustrates par excellence a "deficit" model of young White teachers and their education. In this model, Nell is seen to be ignorant of culture—her own or anyone else's. And formal education, personified by her teacher, is seen to trivialize culture associating it only with a static view of culture-as-ethnicity. The child's teacher and mother can be read as exemplifying the White, middle-class "culture of power," unreflective about its history and privilege.

Other interpretations of Nell's story are possible. Until this assignment, young Nell has apparently not "hyphenated" her American identity. Thus, her teacher has posed an inauthentic problem. Like the child, Nell's mother has not thought of herself in terms of her ancestry and is similarly nonplussed. Yet Nell sets out to fulfill that assignment by creating a good story. If, as the assignment assumes, culture resides in narrative and history, then understanding culture requires not only reason, but also imagination. In that sense, "faking being from Poland" is only marginally different from crafting a story tied more closely to "fact." As we listen to Nell's story, we wonder along with her—What is culture? How do individuals gain access to it? Is culture a label for a group of people? Is culture "one to a customer"? What does culture have to do with history? What does it have to do with literary imagination? What do our cultural stories tell us about others and ourselves? What does culture mean—to the little girl? To the young teacher remembering her schooling? To the profession she is joining?

---

[1]Except for Susan Florio-Ruane and Julie deTar, all book club participants are referred to by pseudonyms.

## OUR PROFESSION, OUR SELVES

For more than two decades I have taught on a sylvan midwestern campus bounded by the state capital, sprawling suburbs, and small farms. Until recently, I also lived in the comfortable cocoon of the university town and worked with teachers much like myself—mostly Euro-American, English-speaking, female, and from middle income backgrounds. Those old enough to remember Lortie's (1975) study of the profession (written before some of my current students were born) will note that my students and I differ very little from the previous generation he described. Like them, we are outwardly homogeneous and also assume a common core of values and beliefs about the role of school in society and the nature of teaching and learning. In our unquestioned sameness we rarely wonder about the differences that our common language, gender, skin color, or social class might mask. Nor do we ask why other faces and voices are not present among us. Our professional education has not forced these questions.

As members of the so-called "mainstream," the preponderance of US teachers find themselves culturally isolated from their pupils who are increasingly from more recent, non-European immigrant backgrounds and lower income families (Chavez Chavez & O'Donnell, 1998; Ferdman, 1990, 1991; Gay, 1993). Perhaps what is most significant about this situation is not how new it is, but how old it is. We could look back to the turn of the last century and also find a homogeneous teaching force serving a linguistically diverse and economically disadvantaged populace. We could similarly find ethnic diversity and the stratification of U.S. society in part by reference to racial, ethnic, and linguistic characteristics. What is astonishing is how little that picture of education has changed in what has otherwise been an astounding century of change in other arenas. Despite transformation of other aspects of society during the 20th century, the mill of public education mostly grinds on. In Lortie's terms, "reaffirmation" rather than "reform" remains the dynamic as successive generations enter our classrooms and profession.

Why does U.S. education look as it does? The answer to that question has in part to do with the profession of teaching. According to Lortie, several factors of self-selection enable the teaching profession's closed, conservative nature. First, teaching is attractive to people who liked school and experienced an "apprenticeship" to teaching as pupils. Second, young women often choose teaching because it offers time flexibility and a calendar compatible with childrearing. And third, many teach because they identify with parents or other significant adults who were also teachers. It seems that our reasons for wanting to teach are tied to a sense of "the way teaching is," and to that extent, beginners know a great deal about teaching before they begin professional education. One can see at a glance how these deciding factors militate against change in the profession. Moreover, embedded in the story of who teaches is another story of who does not teach and why. Noting that U.S. education's history of racial segregation extends to teachers, Kailin (1999) describes teaching as a "raced" profession. Given its history, she notes that

> when we are speaking of a teaching force that just "happens" to be ninety percent white, we must also confront the other aspect of this reality—which is that these people became "white" in a context of white supremacy. In considering the situation of white teachers teaching students of color, an examination of social context is critical. (p. 83)

As we near the retirements of post-war baby boomers, our nation's small contingent of teachers of color is actually declining. We in teacher education mostly scratch our heads in puzzlement as we are yearly urged to step up recruitment of minority teacher candidates. Why, we wonder, is teaching not a profession of choice among young men and women of color? What limited research we have on this question tells us that there are multiple factors at play in teaching's lack of diversity. Some are more within the profession's power to change than are others. And all of these factors suggest that recruitment is a necessary but insufficient effort in achieving a more richly diverse profession.

Delpit (1995) interviewed teachers of color about their experiences as beginning and experienced members of the profession. Many cited teacher education as an impediment to becoming or remaining a teacher. Informants told Delpit, for example, that their university classes did not welcome stories of their learning, their values, or their reasons for wanting to teach. In addition, teachers of color saw and heard their own ethnic groups stereotyped in class discussions and reading assignments, even when their mostly White professors attempted to teach liberally about "cultural diversity." Many felt invisible or ignored, treated not as individuals but as prototypes of minority groups. As such teachers and textbooks spoke for and about them, oversimplifying and stereotyping the cultural experiences they brought to teaching.

Galindo and Olguin (1998) interviewed teachers of Latino heritage and reported similar findings. In a related study, Kuchar (1999) studied high school students' career selection and identified similar experiences among ethnically and linguistically diverse high school students. Many did not identify themselves as people with something to teach. Some wanted to teach but could not see in the teaching career a reflection of their values and goals. The stability of the U.S. teaching force reflects and reinforces patterns of inequality in our society. The absence of language minority teachers and teachers of color is a profound loss for the profession on many levels, not least of which is the resulting impoverishment of the knowledge base for teaching. Absent the insight, knowledge, and imagination of diverse educators, we cannot shape a powerful profession that serves a democratic and pluralistic nation.

Several contextual factors seem within teacher education's grasp to change in support of a more diverse teaching force. Students of color and those speaking a first language other than English need access to academic success and higher education. As Kuchar (1999) observes, all students need the chance to experience school learning as a cognitive apprenticeship in the profession. And, ultimately, youngsters and prospective teachers need to see and learn from teachers and teacher educators of color. To create these conditions, we surely need recruitment of a more diverse teaching force. But recruitment depends on the school experiences of youngsters and, hence, on the education of teachers currently in practice. Recruitment is an empty gesture if youngsters do not see teaching as a viable career or if, on arrival, preservice teachers find that they must shed their personal, cultural narratives in order to become educators. Making culture a more central concept in the texts and contexts of teacher education is the focus of this book. Although this is a broad topic, the settings in which I have tried to examine it are considerably narrower. I have worked on creating and studying transformative contexts in which beginning and experienced teachers might learn about culture.

## ABOUT THIS BOOK

One of the ways I have tried to approach culture in my teaching is by reading autobiographical literature with my students. Without confusing such reading with the pulse-quickening experience of immersion into diverse communities and classrooms, reading autobiographies by authors of diverse backgrounds is a first step. The authors of this literature are powerful interlocutors. And, in their conversational responses to those writers and texts, teachers can awaken aspects of their own experiences of culture, especially those that influence their work as educators. By introducing and researching teacher-led book discussions of ethnic literature, I have tried to investigate ethnic autobiography as a genre from which teachers might learn about culture, literacy, and education in their own and others' lives. Drawing on research on children's book clubs (McMahon & Raphael with Goatley & Pardo, 1997), I also wanted to study peers' reading, writing, and talk about literature as a context for teacher development. Specifically, I wondered if this conversation and literature-based work might be sustainable and foster teachers' comprehension and critical thinking.

I pursued these questions in three related projects: The Future Teachers' Autobiography Club (1993–1994), a course called, "Culture, Literacy, and Autobiography" (1995), and the Literary Circle Study Group (1996–1998). As mentioned earlier, the club for future teachers took the form of monthly dinner and book discussion. I hosted the dinners and joined in the club's far-ranging and often intense conversations. However, I also stepped back to analyze them with the help of Julie deTar, a student member who subsequently became my research colleague. Julie and I found that reading this literature was generative of talk about culture in the book club. But we also found that such conversation was difficult to sustain, particularly when we approached topics on which participants disagreed or about which there was fear or uncertainty (Florio-Ruane & deTar, 1995).

Trying to find ways to support book clubs with curriculum and instruction, I subsequently designed a course for experienced literacy teachers called, "Culture, Literacy, and Autobiography" and taught it in the fall of 1995. A centerpiece of this course, too, was reading and discussing autobiographies dealing with language, culture, and education. In developing the course, I drew on research that Taffy Raphael and her colleagues had undertaken on children's peer-led book clubs (e.g., Raphael, Goatley, McMahon, & Woodman, 1995). Raphael's research found that book clubs, assisted by instruction and responsive writing, could enhance students' comprehension. In adapting Raphael et al.'s book club pedagogy to teacher education, I attempted to provide some limited curricular and instructional support for club members as they struggled with unfamiliar, often challenging literature.

When the course ended, its members remained together in a voluntary club called the Literary Circle. With its formation, the participating teachers gradually assumed more power and responsibility for the group— choosing its name, selecting a place to meet, identifying autobiographies for us to read, and shaping the conversations. Spanning 2 years, 26 books, and as many conversations, members of the Literary Circle experienced an unusually sustained relationship with their colleagues and literature. During that period, Taffy Raphael, several graduate research assistants, and I studied the book clubs and teachers' experience of them as participant observers (Florio-Ruane, Raphael, Glazier, McVee, & Wallace, 1997; Glazier et al., 2000). The sustained nature of this experience and its teacher-led quality made Literary Circle a rich forum within which to study culture and teachers' learning about it.

What made the various book clubs different from other kinds of teacher education in which I have participated was their focus on autobiography, and their emphasis on learning by talk with peers about compelling adult literature. The book clubs can be thought of as small communities of practice (Lave & Wenger, 1991), in which participants are responsible to and for one another's learning. My role in these clubs merged participation and inquiry. For this reason, this book blends personal narrative with analysis and description of ways we explored culture in the stories we told one another and in our responses to published autobiographies. It focuses on two related ideas: (a) autobiography can be a site of teacher learning about culture, and (b) conversation plays an important role in that learning. Thus, autobiography and conversation may be useful ways for teachers to construct their own learning about culture and, in so doing, participate in the transformation of learning in our profession.

# Turning Inward
# to Begin
# Cultural Inquiry

One Sunday morning at the time when I was planning the Future Teachers Autobiography Club, a question on the front page of the Book Review section of the *New York Times* caught my attention: "Where," asked writer Gay Talese (1993), "are the Italian-American novelists?" Like Talese, my ethnic heritage is southern Italian, and my great grandparents came to the United States during the late 19th century, when immigration from eastern and southern Europe was at its peak (Steinberg, 1989). Yet it never occurred to me to wonder why so few of my forebears wrote and published narratives in America. In his essay, Talese wondered why relatively few Italian Americans view their lives as resources for literature. His explanation turned in part on the experience of those Italians from the south, who immigrated to the United States in greatest number. They traditionally valued privacy and did not tell all to strangers. This was a fact of their social and political life, formed in the multiple and repeated conquests of their region and their subsequent economic exploitation by more powerful northern neighbors. Of his ancestors and their American-born offspring Talese wrote,

> Not to protect the privacy of your family from the potential exploitation of your
> prose would have been considered unpardonable within our ethnic group, which

**1**

was overwhelmingly of southern Italian origin and which was still influenced, even a generation or two after our parents' or grandparents' arrival in America, by that Mediterranean region's ancient exhortations regarding prudence, family honor and the safeguarding of secrets. A region that for 2,000 years had been conquered and reconquered by despots of every imaginable variety and vice is a region with an implicit history of caution and with a people united in the fear of being found out. (Talese, 1993, p. 23)

I was intrigued by this explanation. It resonated with my upbringing in a second generation Italian American household where it was rare to discuss (much less write about) one's problems or strong emotions outside the embrace of family. I can recall my mother hastily closing the kitchen windows when the dinner table talk among my parents and grandparents turned from casual banter to more serious subjects—people's health or marital problems, for instance, or the complex interethnic politics of our church and community. But as a child it did not occur to me that this behavior was anything but universal. And to suggest, as Talese did in his essay, that it might have had something to do with cultural history surely did not occur to my family and me. Finally, that this cultural history and its attendant beliefs and practices might help to shape the work of immigrant offspring was a new idea. Until now I had given this aspect of my socialization very little thought although, as a budding researcher, I had studied and written about the dinner table talk of other people's Italian American families (Shultz, Florio, & Erickson, 1982). Pondering my family's private volubility and public guardedness, I began to speculate that growing up in such a setting might account for my research preferences. I enjoy the give and take of conversation but prefer the somewhat distanced role of "participant observer." I am far more comfortable writing about other people and their stories than I am writing about my own. This, it appears, is a condition I share with other Italian Americans.

Writing elsewhere about what he calls "creative nonfiction," Talese confesses to similar preferences, explaining that for the first part of his writing career journalism suited him well. Talese credits hours spent listening to the stories told by customers in his parents' clothing store with honing his skill in "eavesdropping" and sparking his interest in other people's stories. This was apparently good preparation for a career in journalism, writing, in his words, from "the perspective and sensibilities of a small town American outsider" (Talese & Lounsberry, 1996). Talese's parents took pains to make their clothing store inviting to its mostly upscale female customers. As he describes it, his mother "welcomed these

women into her shop as if it were her home" (p. 3), sending him off to fetch tea or soda for them and refusing to interrupt their talk, even when the telephone rang. The women warmed to this welcome and, in the intimacy of the fitting room, talked about difficult issues both personal and political. Of course a young boy would listen, and of this listening the writer says,

> indeed, in the decades since I have left home, during which time I have retained a clear memory of my eavesdropping youth and the women's voices that gave it expression, it seems to me that many of the social and political questions that have been debated in America in the second half of the twentieth century—the role of religion in the bedroom, racial equality, women's rights, the advisability of films and publications featuring sex and violence—all were discussed in my mother's boutique as I grew up during the war and postwar years of the 1940's. (pp. 3–4).

Like Talese, I grew up hearing adults' stories, although mine were told and heard in the home—folding laundry, cooking a meal, weeding the garden, at the dinner table. These stories helped me to learn where I come from and where I stand. As such, they organized, for better and for worse, how I made my way as a student and, ultimately, as a teacher. And they likely drew me to educational anthropology. I thought that my careful listening as an ethnographer would yield stories of the cultural experiences of other people. What I did not acknowledge was the extent to which my recounting of other people's experiences was seen through the lens of my own. Talese's dressing room insight about the interweaving of the self, the other, and the society in which they come together pushed me to think about how listening and re-telling of stories might be about far more than I had assumed either as a child or as a researcher.

## ETHNOGRAPHIC STORIES OF SELF

Although all research is, in some sense autobiographical (Phelps, 1988), autobiography is not always the appropriate goal of scholarship. Erickson (1996) points out that 25 years ago, the ethnographer's aim to describe others and their points of view, what he calls the naming function or "Adam's work," was considered novel, even controversial in social science. Yet, since then, new controversies have arisen within qualitative research about the very presumption that an ethnographer can or should speak for and about others. Of this Erickson (1996) says:

ethnographic realism is no longer credible to many of us within ethnography itself. We have come to realize that the so-called "participant observer" is only minimally participating, and is mostly outside the social gravity within which the "observed" live. (p. 7).

To redress this problem, researchers can take on what Erickson calls, "Eve's task," moving from the role of a participant observer to that of an "observant participant," for whom research is personal and relational. Yet, while arguing for a more revealing portrayal of the ethnographer in ethnography, we can go too far, producing autobiography rather than ethnography. Erickson illustrates with the following joke overheard at an anthropology conference:

> *Question*: What did the informant say to the postmodern ethnographer who was interviewing her?
>
> *Answer*: Enough about you. Let's talk about me. (p. 12)

Among other contemporary anthropologists (e.g., Clifford, 1988; Rosaldo, 1989), Erickson argues for balancing Adam's and Eve's tasks— for trying to understand and describe others' lives while acknowledging how we inevitably do this in ways mediated by our own autobiographies. Behar (1993) makes a similar point in her ethnographic study, *Translated Woman*, in which the story of her key informant, a Mexican woman named Esperanza, is jointly constructed by and serves the authorial purposes of both researcher and informant. And Behar further notes that although this idea might have been a new one to contemporary ethnographers, it is not new to feminist cultural scholars, for whom Eve's task has been a long-standing, if underappreciated, one (Behar & Gordon, 1995).

Despite the obvious risk of solipsistic self-absorption, the interplay of autobiography and ethnography was newly appealing as I pondered Talese's Sunday morning query. For years, as teacher educator, I have extolled the virtue of teachers considering the relationship between children's cultural identities and their learning of literacy. Yet I have not urged teachers to consider this issue in their own lives, especially as it affects their relationships with youngsters and their families. And, most disturbing, I have also not examined this issue in my own practice. What is the role of autobiography in coming of age both as a literate person and an educator? How does our primary socialization in family and community influence our work as teachers and students? Why is it difficult to talk, much less write, about these issues as they have shaped us as teachers and learners?

I am, of course, neither the only nor the first practitioner to ask such questions. And it is important to note that some educational scholars appropriately critique exclusive reliance on such introspection among privileged Euro-American teachers as self-indulgent, a detour away from the profoundly troubling (and threatening) issues of racism and economic inequality. Sleeter (1994), for example, points out that when Euro-American teachers "tap our own ethnic immigrant experience for guidance," we are apt to reinforce unquestioningly the dominant ideology that, in her words,

> the United States is a nation of immigrants: our ancestors all came here to seek opportunity. Ethnic identity is a choice, something to add onto a common American identity. Ethnicity is a sidebar, no longer relevant to our relationships with social institutions, which are color-blind and ethnic-blind. (p. 6)

Such an outcome of autobiographic work by Euro-American teachers might merely serve to reinforce what Steinberg (1989) calls the "ethnic myth" that cultural background informs and shapes behavior. In Steinberg's analysis, this view does not consider how ethnic identity itself is socially formed and how, in the United States, that identity is forged in a crucible where language, culture, race, class, gender, economics, history, and politics meet. Absent an examination of our own and others' ethnic experience, it is difficult to engage, for example, the topic of racism. Without examining one's own history and learning, teachers' study of culture can be an exercise in mere "tolerance," what Nieto (1994) calls the "low level acceptance of surface feature differences." One can be "tolerant" without having to risk revealing biases to oneself or others. But to reach a place of "affirmation, solidarity, and critique," learners must probe more deeply their own formations and their relationship with others. To accomplish this kind of cultural understanding can be risky, but Nieto notes that learners must "work and struggle with one another, even if it is sometimes difficult and challenging" (p. 9).

## REMEMBERING ETHNICITY

The social construction of "ethnicity" can be traced in the experiences of individuals and groups. In this way, ethnicity is a researchable question.

Counter to the tendency to romanticize immigrant experience and the culturally diverse "huddled masses" arriving on U.S. shores, ethnicity can and should be studied as a social and historical process. In Steinberg's (1989) terms:

> by its very nature, ethnicity involves ways of thinking, feeling, and acting that constitute the essence of culture. That ethnic groups have unique cultural character can hardly be denied. The problem, however, is that culture does not exist in a vacuum; nor it is fixed or unchanging. On the contrary, culture is in constant flux and is integrally a part of a larger social process. The mandate for social inquiry, therefore, is that ethnic patterns should not be taken at face value, but must be related to the larger social matrix in which they are embedded. (p. 1)

Making ethnicity the subject of rational inquiry de-romanticizes the concept and focuses on the ways that we all participate in the social construction of identity. In a country whose history is marked both by transformation in immigrants' life chances and by persistent inequality and racism, it is important to shine the light of reasoned inquiry on the "ethnic myth."

Yet this important work can easily be experienced as distancing, especially to students and teachers for whom the ethnic past is, in the words of Nell's mother, "a long time ago." For this reason, the study of culture also needs to be made personal. Without experiencing culture as a social process in which I participate, it is difficult for me to understand it as part of my inheritance and formation. Moreover, it is difficult, absent this understanding, for me to awaken to my participation in this process as a teacher and a citizen.

It was the hint of this awakening that captured my imagination when I read Talese's question. It sparked recollection and reflection, situating my family and me in terms of a process of coming to be Italian Americans. Subsequently, as I hope this book will illustrate, it also helped me see how that experience is a difficult and complex one. My forebears were both risk-taking and guarded. And, on entry to the United States, they joined other immigrants in a social and political transformation that was of great benefit to them. However, on reaping that benefit, they (and I) acquired new values and attitudes. Becoming "Americans," we "bought the line" of racism and presumed social inequality.[1] Thus, we experienced loss and

---

[1] I thank Mike Rose for urging me to follow this idea in my thinking and writing.

forgetting, especially as we participated in the recreation of inequality on the basis of race and social class. This, too, is the story of my ethnic inheritance, and accessing it for critical reflection is exceedingly difficult. The formation of European immigrants and their offspring is an uncomfortable one, easily romanticized, understandably rationalized. In order to think about the topic critically, we need to be touched emotionally by it. Perhaps for this reason, educators and theorists of multicultural education are turning increasingly to narrative and dialogue to study teaching and culture (e.g., Athanases, 1998; Casey, 1993; Clandinnin & Connelly, 1987; Conle, 1997; Phillion, 1999; Proefriedt, 1989/1990).

Anthropologist Michael Fischer (1986) asserts that "ethnicity is a deeply rooted emotional component of identity" which, in his words, is

> often transmitted less through cognitive language or learning (to which sociology has almost entirely restricted itself) than through processes analogous to the dreaming and transference of psychoanalytic encounter. (p. 195)

Part of accessing ethnic identity depends on remembering, both as recalling and reconstructing. This is a process of self-discovery that can also lead to the discovery of others (Au, 1995). Remembering involves not only recalling previously known facts but crafting narratives on the basis of learned information. The task of understanding is one that involves both reason and imagination to construct a past whereby one can situate and understand a present. This abstract idea is illustrated in the following excerpt from the poem, "The Dream," which is included in an anthology of Italian-American women's writing compiled and edited by Helen Barolini (1985). In it, the poet Michelle Belluomini (cited in Barolini, 1985, p. 100), learns about herself by visiting a forgotten place and listening across time and language to echoes of a grandmother's voice.

back in the old neighborhood
cautiously picking my way among
abandoned houses and broken
sidewalks
I am trying to follow my grandmother
but clumsily, I fear I will fall
she shouts encouragement to me in

Italian
she climbs a rope ladder to the attic
words float from her mouth like water

Paula Salvio, a teacher and scholar with whom I share ethnic heritage, sent me an excerpt of Barolini's book containing these verses. Reading Belluomini's words stirred awareness of the contradictions and conflicts I felt in forging out of my Italian-American girlhood a woman's life and work radically different from, yet powerfully entwined with, the values, beliefs, and practices of my grandmothers and mother. The verse evokes images of my own family's move upward. It shows what is broken, what is lost—voice, contact, and connection with the past—loss of one mother's tongue for another. This past is mysterious, magical—I cannot parse my grandmother's floating words. The old neighborhood is also abandoned—a place where, as immigrants, my forebears were often silent, secretive, judgmental, and afraid of strangers who looked or spoke differently from themselves. I recall holding my grandmother's hand as we walked to the butcher shop on "the avenue." I also recall the jerk of my arm as she pulled me across the street thus avoiding the dark-skinned man walking toward us. Perhaps, as part of leaving the old neighborhood, the speaker in Belluomini's "Dream" becomes less afraid. Her grandmother's shouts of encouragement, difficult to understand, may not be to follow her into the dark and musty attic. Perhaps the old immigrant woman, herself a traveler, is encouraging her granddaughter to continue to risk the journey outward.

Ethnic identity operates largely outside conscious awareness. It is a social construction shared by people rather than genetically given at birth. In Au's (1995) words, "the use of the term ethnicity here is not based on the suspect biological factors typically associated with the term race. Instead, ethnicity refers to groups with shared histories and cultural knowledge" (p. 2). Given this definition, generalizations about people on the basis of ethnicity are complex and can be misleading. Au notes that because the conditions for the social construction of a group's identity are variable and subject to change over time,

anthropologists and other social scientists acknowledge that there is great variability among members of any particular ethnic or cultural group due, for example, to differences in social class, time of immigration, or individual preferences (p. 2).

Thus, it is exceedingly difficult to use the concept of culture to understand or account for identity in any neatly deterministic way. It is less a defining characteristic than a process. It is what we do to identify ourselves as members of groups holding common heritage, language, or social values.

## REPRESENTING CULTURE AND ETHNIC IDENTITY

Ethnicity synthesizes personality and performance in the expression of self. When Schieffelin and Ochs (1986) studied the language learning of youngsters across cultures, for example, they described socialization into language and culture as a process of "interactional display (covert or overt) to a novice of expected ways of thinking, feeling, and acting" (p. 2). These expectations are communicated within social contexts and relationships such that the youngster not only internalizes ways of speaking (or feeling or acting), but also recognition of the settings, activities, and social relationships in which these are appropriate.

Following the social psychological theories of George Herbert Mead (1956), Schieffelin and Ochs argue that youngsters, from the very start of their lives, negotiate a sense of cultural identity in interaction with others in particular social contexts. As such they are not passive recipients of culture, but active co-creators of it, reflexively shaping and being shaped by ordinary relationships and activities. In fact, for George Herbert Mead it was the construction of identity in and through encounters with others that rescued the idea of socialization from the tidy, suffocating reproduction of culture to an occasion for its transformation and renewal with each new life and generation. In these analyses despite its limitations as definer of self, ethnicity remains an important component of our life history and provides background knowledge influencing how we behave and make sense of others' behavior. Because it is deeply penetrated by language and is taught and learned implicitly in the course of everyday life, ethnicity, like language, tends to be taken for granted unless we are called upon to make it explicit for purposes of differentiating ourselves from others. This might happen when we travel or meet newcomers or perhaps when we have access to the history of our extended families. It often happens when we narrate our life stories in which, necessarily, "the question of the self's identity becomes the question of the self's location in the world" (Graham, 1991, p. 31).

Unfortunately, research on culture has not always served us well as a genre by which to experience culture. Literary scholar Mary Louise Pratt (1986) registers her disappointment with social science's ways of representing the experience of culture as follows:

> There are strong reasons why field ethnographers so often lament that their ethnographic writings leave out or hopelessly impoverish some of the most important knowledge they have achieved, including the self-knowledge. For the lay person such as myself, the main evidence of a problem is the simple fact that ethnographic writing tends to be surprisingly boring. How, one asks constantly, could such interesting people doing such interesting things produce such dull books? What did they have to do to themselves? (pp. 32–33)

Pratt locates the problem in the shift in point of view required when one writes to explain or describe others. To adopt the scientist's outsider perspective in the name of objectivity and rigor in description, an ethnographer loses the insider's perspective on change, conflict, contradiction and transformation. Thus, in attempting to describe or explain cultural experience objectively, authors often compromise the narrative power of their own and others' experience of the process of living culture. She writes that

> in terms of its own metaphors, the scientific position of speech is that of an observer fixed on the edge of a space, looking in and/or down upon what is other. Subjective experience, on the other hand, is spoken from a moving position already within or down in the middle of things, looking and being looked at, talking and being talked at. To convert fieldwork, via field notes, into formal ethnography requires a tremendously difficult shift from the latter discursive position (face to face with the other) to the former. Much must be left behind in the process. (p. 33).

Social scientific description compresses information and, in so doing, can wring from it the unique, the particular, the conflictual, and the contradictory.[2] Yet it does this in the spirit of rigorous theorizing about human nature. The shift from participant to describer inevitably changes our perspective and hence our descriptions. This being the case, any description

---

[2]I am grateful to Sarah Michaels for pointing this out in a conference she organized in celebration of the work and career of Courtney Cazden.

of culture should be read with attention to the limits of its point of view. But texts offered as scientific bear particular scrutiny because of their claim to "authoritative knowledge" (Cherryholmes, 1988). Much of what currently comprises the study of culture in teacher education paradoxically works at cross-purposes with the experience of culture. Relying primarily on generalizations drawn from social science, its oral and written discourse leaves out the detail as well as the drama of lived experience. The reader sees others as frozen or lifeless and herself as aloof from cultural forces shaping identity and life chances. To the degree that they bypass or subordinate narrative in describing cultural experience, such accounts drain conflict, contradiction, motive, agency, and moral content from human experience

A paradox of fieldwork in anthropology is that one must become vulnerably engaged with another to learn about him or her and that, in so doing, one also learns enormously about oneself. This paradox also occurs in learning to teach, especially in multicultural settings. Here, according to Bernardo Ferdman (1990), "the first step . . . involves turning inward. Before helping others to do so, one must initially explore one's own values and attitudes about ethnic diversity, as well as one's degree of awareness of the role culture plays in one's own formation" (p. 366). We tend to look at our own lives in nuanced ways and are not caricatures to ourselves. Like autobiographers, who make literature of their lives, we know that our "self" is uniquely crafted in the context of our relationships and circumstances. In the same spirit we may, by autobiography, come to know our students in more nuanced ways as well. Inward looking works against cultural stereotyping; it also works against the tendency to look at a child's learning out of context. In this way, we begin to see that others are complex individuals whose identities are shaped but not determined by culture.

Calling teachers' study of their own and others' life narratives "threshold autobiography" (p. 288), Salvio (1990) asserts that by crafting, dramatizing, and responding to life narratives, the teacher "initiates a process of reflection and re-construction that places her on the threshold of development." By raising issues of culture and identity in aesthetic ways, readers and authors move from distancing generalization to what Salvio calls representation of "the life of feeling" replete with "conflicts, inconsistencies, questions . . . pain, and desire" (p. 288). Viewed this way, learning to teach multiculturally is not reducible to a set of techniques, procedures, or homilies. Rather, in Chavez Chavez and O'Donnell's (1998) words, multicultural teaching and learning is "idiosyncratic to the contextual *and* processual experiences the teacher and the learner bring *at the moment of engagement*" (p. 13).

Teacher candidates often feel isolated and quite literally helpless when their initial attempts at instructing diverse pupils are met with misunderstanding or resistance. Thus, a cycle begins in which, despite—or perhaps in virtue of their contact with pupils from diverse backgrounds—teacher candidates experience a hardening sense of the difference between "us" and "them." Teachers are encouraged despite their lack of resources to teach in ways that are more inclusive and inviting of participation by all learners. It is not surprising to find them resisting these approaches or making only limited progress with them and ultimately relying on more traditional recitation-based modes of instruction, if only to help them retain or regain a sense of control over their classrooms. This is a problem endemic to teacher education regardless of the background of the teacher candidate. Absent a transformative curriculum for studying culture, students have little to look to except what they have learned about culture at home. And, as is illustrated in the case of my own upbringing, many of us have experienced home lives fostering isolation from difference. In this regard, Banks (1993) notes the following:

> Most students in the United States are socialized within communities that are segregated along racial, ethnic, and social-class lines. Consequently, most American youths have few opportunities to learn firsthand about the cultures of people from different racial, ethnic, cultural, religious, and social-class groups. (pp. 7–8).

Banks critiques both academic and personal knowledge as partial, interest-driven, and unreflective. He argues for a curriculum in which students—and teachers—can learn about culture by means of "transformative" texts. These are texts that, in Banks' words, "challenge mainstream academic knowledge and expand and substantially revise established canons, paradigms, theories, explanations, and research methods" (p. 7). A hallmark of such texts is their reflexive character, their acknowledgment that cultural study is inevitably partial, interest-driven, and value-laden.

Autobiography may serve as one such transformative genre. Of it autobiographer and critic, Jill Ker Conway (1992), writes that it offers readers "chances to enter and inhabit the real world of another person, chances to try on identity and so broaden our own" (p. x). The literary genre blends fiction, personal narrative, history, and cultural description (Stone, 1981). In so doing, it offers access to the individual's unique experience and also places that experience within a social group and historical period (Holte, 1988). And, as a hybrid genre, it mobilizes language both referentially, to convey general information about a culture, and poetically, to foster identification between reader and writer, often across considerable differences in background. Although such identification can be troublesome in that it may obscure genuine inequities among members of different groups in the society, it is also powerful in breaking through the separation that typically is created by textual representations of the other as an object of description. Fischer (1986) says in this regard that, since the concept of "ethnicity" is only really meaningful in the context of difference among groups, it is important to read with an eye toward difference. He sees ethnic autobiography as a powerful text for such reading because it is about the construction of identity in and through contact with others like and different from oneself. He says,

> In thinking about how to read, analyze, and interpret these contemporary autobiographical texts, it occurred to me that the ethnic search is a mirror of the bifocality that has always been a part of anthropological research: seeing others against a background of ourselves, and ourselves against a background of others. The juxtaposing of exotic customs to familiar ones, or the relativizing of taken-for-granted assumptions, has always been the kind of cultural criticism promised by anthropology. This bifocality, or reciprocity of perspective, has become increasingly important in a world of growing interdependence between societies. . . . (p. 199)

Studying cultural narratives may encourage teachers to examine the lives of persons whose backgrounds differ from their own and simultaneously uncover, in Zeichner's (1993) words, "their own cultural identities and reexamine their attitudes toward and beliefs about different ethnocultural groups" (p. 20). In these texts the reader is not merely informed about cultural groups or treated as a spectator of someone else's journey. Rather, she or he is invited into the exploration and encouraged to respond in personal ways. Moreover, in writing autobiography, contemporary authors examine and often challenge the idea that there is a continuous, seamless "I", or self, about whom they are writing. Instead, there is in autobiography a "complex weaving" of selves viewed in terms of the author's multiple experiences in contact with others (Zuss, 1997). Viewed this way, autobiography is a genre that explores identity and the world even as it appears to describe one person's identity in the world. As such, in autobiography, "aspects of memory, referential personal and community history and stories can be grafted with features of fantasy and fiction" (Zuss, 1997, p. 168).

This is both the power and potential limitation of autobiography as a genre for teaching teachers about culture. Its power rests with identification and the possibility of seeing all cultural experience as emergent and relative—including one's own. But there is also a risk that readers will level across experiences and miss the sense in which, due to systemic inequality, some people's efforts to craft identities are greatly limited or complicated by unfairness in their treatment by others. However, to risk identification may well be a first step away from objectifying others and entering their worlds. From here, it may be possible also to assess the particular difficulties others are faced with that would, ordinarily, be outside the teacher's purview. Although speaking of practice in medicine, not teaching, psychiatrist Robert Coles (1989) said in this regard that teaching and learning his profession through literary texts has

> helped my work along by reminding me how complex, ironic, and ambiguous this life can be and that the conceptual categories I learned in psychiatry and psychoanalysis in social science seminars are not the only means by which one might view the world. (p. xvii)

Frustrated with the way I teach beginning teachers about the cultural foundations for literacy, I began to look for alternative texts and contexts. I found intriguing the idea that cultural experience might be accessible to beginning teachers in literature and other artistic renderings of human life. This idea led me to consider other literatures and other arenas for discussion than had been standard in the academic experiences of our beginning teachers. I was intrigued by discussion of ethnic autobiography as an alternate and perhaps more powerful way for teachers to learn about culture in their own and others' lives. The autobiography book clubs described in this book explored the idea that personal narrative might enrich the education of teachers, prompting such questions about their own lives and those of their pupils as the following:

> (1) How is literacy defined in the individual's group and what is its significance? (2) What significance do particular texts have for an individual's cultural identity? (3) How do the particular pedagogical approaches or the texts used for the purposes of literacy in school relate to the learner's motives and sense of identity? (4) What messages does a reading and writing curriculum communicate about the value of the learner's culture? and (5) What relationship does the

learner perceive between the tasks assigned in school and his or her cultural identity? Must the learner change the nature of the self-concept in order to do what is asked? (paraphrased from Ferdman, 1991, pp. 110—111).

Questions like these move teachers to consider what it means to be educated and literate in particular cultural traditions and contexts. Learning that language, identity, education, and culture are inextricably entwined, we may approach the teaching of literacy with greater sensitivity, insight, and imagination.

# CHAPTER 2

# Talking and Thinking About Culture

It is harder to think about culture than it is to talk about it. At best a conceptual moving target, even anthropologists contest its definition (Finnan & Swanson, 2001). Most people would agree that culture is far more than "local color. " It is not merely food, costumes, and festivals. But easily saying what it is not, we struggle to learn what it might be. We can be helped to understand "culture" by looking at ways people have struggled with other "big ideas." In this chapter I want to make three points about culture: first, like other "big ideas" it resists easy definition; second, despite this resistance, our definitional work reveals culture's power as an idea in education; and third, our definitional work involves conversation and story— both acts of imagination. I would like to illustrate these ideas first by turning to a story about another such "big idea," Carver's (1982) short story, "What We Talk about When We Talk about Love."[1] In this story, friends engage in a rambling conversation trying to define love. During this ramble they visit many of love's dimensions, contradictions, complexities, and expressions. Resisting consensus or concise definition, "love," is a concept inviting dialogue, disagreement, metaphor, and narrative.

---

[1]Other social scientists and educators have played on Carver's evocative title. See, for example, Davenport and Presack (1998) and Casella (1999).

## CONVERSATION AND CONCEPTS

Four adults—two couples—are sitting around talking over a bottle of gin. They wander onto the topic of love, and what we learn as we read the story is that each person in the group holds different views of what love might be. Not only are there as many "working definitions" of love as there are people in the group, but individual speakers also seem to hold multiple definitions of love. The conversation Carver crafts demonstrates that something as essential as the idea of love has no essence—it can actually be multilayered and very hard to define. Although everyone at the table is sufficiently confident in their view of love to express it and challenge others' views, each person's representation of love is incomplete. Many of the "working definitions" of love available in participants' talk are in conflict with both our expectations and with the definitions offered by others around the table.

Carver's characters participate in a form of talk we all are accustomed to hearing and doing. This is not an academic exercise or a debate. It is a conversation among friends. As such it unfolds as a series of vignettes told by the participants to illustrate or exemplify what they think love might be. The speakers encircle their emerging topic in a causal, meandering way. Carver says, "There was ice in the bucket on the table. The gin and the tonic water kept going around, and somehow we got on the subject of love." Such informal topic finding is characteristic of friends talking for the sheer pleasure of it, yet Carver shows that such meandering can sometimes lead participants onto very significant ground. In their conversation about love, the members of the group proffer various competing definitions. Love is spiritual to Mel, a former seminarian. But it is violent to his wife, Terri. Describing a lover from her past she says he "loved me so much he tried to kill me." Terri and Mel argue about whether this is, indeed, a proper definition of love. At an apparent impasse, Terri's story dominates for several pages as she recounts further violence in the name of love. As the narrator listens to Terri describe her former lover's eventual violent death, he thinks about his relationship with own wife, Laura, and the very different picture of love it provides. This interior narrative seems calm and ordered, even dispassionate when contrasted with Terri's spoken one:

> Laura is a legal secretary. We'd met in a professional capacity. Before we knew it, it was a courtship. She's thirty-five, three years younger than I am. In addition to being in love, we like each other and enjoy one another's company. She's easy to be with.

Thus, the author draws our attention to Laura. Yet when she at last has an opportunity to speak, she does not mention her own thoughts about love but prompts Terri to continue her narrative about her violent former lover asking "What happened?" Mel, Terri's husband, fields the question, interjecting flatly, "He shot himself in the mouth in his room."

Once again, tension rises as Mel and Terri's disagreement about the meaning of love is spoken. Mel says, "If you call that love, you can have it." "It was love," Terri responds. "Sure it's abnormal in most people's eyes. But he was willing to die for it. He did die for it." To this point, by means of argument and story, the members of the group have defined love in powerfully conflicting ways. For some, it is spiritual, like the love of God for human beings. For others, it is passionate to the point of violence toward the love object and oneself. Still for others, it is something that "happens" spontaneously and without complication and starts with the simplicity of enjoying a person's company. Although there is strain in their talk through these differences, the friends proceed. Although the meaning of love may be in dispute, they appear not to doubt the conversational common ground on which they stand, what McDermott and Tylbor (1983, cited in Tannen, 1989, p. 12) call the "collusion" by which we keep each other engaged in social discourse and make meaning together. Thus, the characters embody dialogue's possibility to sustain engagement in and through difficulty illustrating, in Crapanzano's (1990, cited in Burbules, 1993) words, that dialogue "is a passing through and a going apart . . . a relationship of considerable tension" (p. 15).

"What do any of us really know about love?" Mel asks. " It seems to me we're just beginners at love." He illustrates with yet another story. A physician, he describes being called to the hospital to attend to an elderly couple seriously injured in a gruesome auto accident. As conversations will, this one meanders, and Mel's story is punctuated by asides, some loosely associated with his story (such as joking about wearing seat belts), and others off the topic but pertinent to group's situation (like when and where to have dinner). There is even an apparent conversational detour about how medieval knights may have loved in armor—perhaps evoked by the vulnerability conveyed in the image of an aged couple riding in a car and adding a sense of romance, even gallantry, to his story of the aged couple. Laura again draws the group back asking Mel, "What about the old couple? You didn't finish that story you started." Implicit in her question is the expectation that Mel's long, often interrupted story will somehow make a point about love—the topic that has remained on the conversational floor all evening.

Mel describes how the old man and his wife are finally brought by dint of great medical effort from the brink of death. They are going to pull through. But the old man swaddled in bandages with only holes for his eyes, nose, and mouth does not show relief. Puzzled, Mel talks with him, listening to his voice at the mouth hole cut in his bandages. He learns that the old man is disheartened because he cannot see his beloved. Wrapped like a mummy in his bandages, he cannot turn his head and therefore cannot look at the other mummy lying beside him. "I'm telling you the man's heart was breaking because he couldn't turn his goddamn head and see his goddamn wife." The narrator says, "We all looked at Mel." "Do you see what I'm saying?" asks Mel. There is no reply, but the narrator hints, "Maybe we were a little drunk by then. I know it was hard to keep things in focus." And the evening winds down with talk about what and where to eat, whether or not to call the kids, and what to do when the gin is finished.

The arc of this story is very familiar—we warm to a topic, immerse ourselves in give and take about it, and then re-emerge to think about and do other things. Carver's fiction thereby reveals the ordinary and taken for granted. He shows us people spinning the fabric of conversation with the filaments of personal narrative. The author demonstrates how participants help one another to explore an idea as well as to pass time in one another's company. He also shows that at times this social accomplishment of the ordinary conversation endures conflict and competition. Ultimately, ordinary talk articulates profound aspects of love. What we talk about when we talk about it are life, death, violence, risk, aging, history, ordinary life, chance encounters, friendship, sexual passion, and more. And, if friendship is a kind of love, the conversation itself embodies aspects of love at work.

## METAPHORS AND MEANINGS

For Carver's characters, this conversation arises informally, for its own sake rather than in the service of some explicit educational goal. If we were to question the "use" of such talk, we might conclude that the point of the conversation was precisely the meandering of thought and speech around this complicated idea. Conversation exists for its own survival— and the conviviality of passing the time engaged in making and opposing ideas among friends. It also appeals to educators as a tool for learning that is authentically engaging, democratic, and fosters exploration of complicated ideas (Burbules, 1993; Chavez Chavez & O'Donnell, 1998). I dwell on Carver's short story because it offers a thumbnail sketch conversation and story as a means to examine a complex and important concept. The speakers spin stories to make their points and reveal themselves to one another in particular ways. They engage in acts of creative imagination to negotiate both a conversation and a concept. Central to this creative work is their use of metaphor.

"Metaphor," according to Lentriccia and McLaughlin (1990), is thought of by many literary critics as "the master, or central" figure of speech in literature. It can be defined as a "compressed analogy" that involves "a transfer of meaning from the word that properly possesses it to another word which belongs to some shared category of meaning" (p. 83). This transfer of meaning is a powerful process that reveals complexity. Although metaphor is used in its heightened form as a literary figure of speech, we also learn metaphorically in everyday life. This means, as Dewey asserted and is revisited in Jackson's (1998) study of his aesthetics, that we use metaphor and the literary imagination as we go about the mundane business of "making sense" in daily life and as we go about the perhaps less mundane business of theorizing. Metaphors familiar to contemporary educational researchers, for example, would be the instructional "scaffold" (Bruner, 1974) and the Vygotskian (1978) "zone" of proximal development— two familiar, related images that help us understand and speak about the dynamic process whereby development is supported by and occurs within interactions of more and less knowledgeable others.

Carver's characters use metaphor in stories of their own experience to reveal what love means. Of course it can be argued that Carver was a fiction writer and love a "many-splendored thing" about which the heart wisely leads the head. When we turn our attention to businesslike concepts such as "literacy" or "culture," we tend to want more literal, systematic, and rational means to fix a precise definition that might inform policy and practice. Yet precise definitions do not come easily. Haggling over those proffered in our research, we begin to feel quite a bit like Carver's friends, telling stories of "what literacy or culture is like " in order to try to define it. In this spirit, cultural psychologist, Sylvia Scribner (1984), advanced metaphor as a way to reveal the complexity of a concept in her essay, "Literacy in Three Metaphors." She noted that when teachers, researchers or policymakers study literacy, there is a tendency to expect that

> Literacy is a kind of reality that educators should be able to grasp and explain, or, expressed in more classical terms, that literacy has an "essence" that can be

captured through some Aristotelian-like enterprise. By a rational process of discussion and analysis, the "true" criterial components of literacy will be identified, and these in turn can become the target of education for literacy. (p. 7)

Understanding literacy, Scribner argued, might better be served by opening ourselves to examining the "differing points of view" about literacy's meaning; the different experiences of literacy practiced and described by people in particular contexts, historical periods, activities, and societies.

Scribner was alert to the complexity of the idea of "literacy" in large part because her research was cross-cultural. Scribner had many occasions to see what literacy was like in unfamiliar places, and this experience not only introduced alternate metaphors of literacy to her but occasioned her thinking about those metaphors she applied and took for granted in more familiar settings and activities. To illustrate, she offered several ways of seeing of literacy metaphorically—literacy as adaptation to life's functional requirements; as power with which to transform the conditions of one's life; and as a state of grace, the refinement of human experience in literacy and the sacredness of text. She thus urged inquiry not into literacy's "essence," but into the hows, whys, and wherefores of its representation.

It is worth noting that Scribner's essay was addressed to educational planners. Her aesthetic approach to researching a concept seems far afield from the blunt, rationalized language of policy. Yet exploring hard to define concepts like literacy (or culture) in terms of our and others' metaphors may, in fact, get us closer to the assumptions, beliefs, and passions underlying researchers' terms, methods, and findings. For "culture," as for "literacy," it is important to uncover and express our metaphors precisely because they underlie our educational theories, policies, and practices. Recalling Nell, with whom this book began, we can ask what metaphors for culture are implicit in her story. What does culture mean to her that it must be exotic or dramatic? What does it mean to that she felt it could or needed to be "faked"? What Nell talks about when she talks about culture reveals tacit knowledge, beliefs, and values. And what Nell thinks and learns about "culture" colors her work as a teacher just as surely as what she thinks about "literacy" does.

*Culture*, like love and literacy, is a commonplace term in daily life and, perhaps even more so, in the lives of people learning to teach. Both novice and experienced teachers who took part in the autobiography book clubs used the term *culture* in ordinary talk. They also heard professors and administrators tell them to appreciate and respect the cultural differences among pupils. But in our conversations about culture, particularly in response to provocative literature, book club participants confronted the challenge of saying what they and others "meant by it." This is illustrated in an analysis of book club conversation by Mary McVee (cited in Glazier et al., 2000). McVee grew up on a ranch in Montana, and she participated in a book club discussion of Conway's (1989) book, *The Road from Coorain*, with teachers who had grown up in Michigan. Coorain is a sheep ranch in the Australian outback, and Conway's family is forced to leave the family ranch because of a severe drought.

Coorain is a central metaphor in Conway's autobiography of her life in rural and urban Australia and her coming of age as a woman and scholar. The book club members talked about Coorain drawing on their own lived experiences. Several teachers in the group grew up on dairy farms in Michigan. Because their families did not have to grow their own food for the dairy cattle, the teachers did not share Conway's desperate experience of watching livestock starve to death because of drought. However, they shared the experience of growing up in a wide expanse of land and livestock and of a family's dependence on nature for their livelihood. As the conversation unfolded, dairy farm narratives predominated. I was participating in the book club as the instructor in the course in which it occurred. Having experienced neither dairy farm nor ranch life, I was not alert to the power and nuance of these metaphors. Feeling that we were getting bogged down talking about farming, I made what is a common instructional move (and what was in this case an instructional mistake). I urged the group to push on in terms of consensus and generalization. I asked them think about two issues: what these varied experiences might have in common, and how the stories of these experiences might illuminate a theme with which Conway was concerned.

As I made this move, McVee simmered. Having grown up on a ranch and lived through her family's near loss of its land because of drought, she was frustrated by the group's press toward a sense of common understanding (i.e., most of us grew up on farms). She also understood that such consensus might, in fact, obscure rather than illuminate the themes within Conway's book. McVee wanted the group to acknowledge that "a ranch is not a dairy farm" and begin from that acknowledgment to struggle with the differences as a starting point for talking about their responses to Coorain and the drought as central metaphors in Conway's autobiography (McVee, cited in Glazier et al., 2000).

Metaphors challenge us to try to say what we mean. And if we struggled with Conway's agrarian one, we surely struggled with the complex concepts that metaphor was meant to illuminate. Like Carver's characters, our effort to put words to culture in discussion of works of literature (and in our own stories told in conversation) made the concept more edgy and complicated. The term was shot through with dilemmas and even danger as speakers told about culture's manifestations in experiences with youngsters resistant to their efforts at teaching, or parents and grandparents who were illiterate, or teachers' roles as school authorities—and how these roles imposed new power and responsibility on them. In short, no homiletic definition of culture (as no such definition of love) would be full enough to hold the richness and complexity of the phenomenon as lived. Instead, the stories we told and read captured aspects of culture's meaning and complexity. Thus, conversation and narrative became central to understanding, especially if we could risk looking at difference and disagreement.

## THE ELUSIVENESS
## OF CULTURE IN TEACHERS' EDUCATION

Studying our metaphors for culture is difficult. Either, culture is everywhere and therefore as *The New York Times* recently proclaimed, "means anything, bad as well as good" (Rothstein, 1999), or it is so remote as to be irrelevant. The concept of culture, when applied to education, is similarly elusive. On one hand, it peppers most educational discourse concerning equity in practices and curricula. Yet it all but disappears in the major policies and practices of public education in our time. Since at least the end of the last century, schools have been places where a shared "American" identity was expected to be forged (Greene, 1994). Given this socializing mission, it has not been a priority of teacher education to, in Delpit's (1995) words, "foster inquiry into who our students really are or encourage teachers to develop links to the often rich home lives of students" (p. 179). Instead, students' nonschool lives and associations are "checked at the door," as schools focus fervently on academic learning and attainment of American political values as if these were independent of ethnic, linguistic, or social identity. Thus, pupils and teachers experience what Barrera (cited in Walker & MacGillivray, 1999) calls a "culturalectomy".

Educational culturalectomy is most clearly visible in the experiences of students of color and those who speak a first language other than English, who rarely find their images reflected in the texts and contexts of school. Some scholars argue that such youngsters experience not only an "ectomy" of home language and culture, but also a "transplant" of mainstream, or what some scholars of color have called "whitestream," cultural values and practices.[2] This being the case, our schools better reflect and respect the experience of youngsters who are middle class, whose first language is English, and who are the descendents of immigrants from western Europe. However, this unequal situation does not mean that the youngsters of the privileged, so-called "mainstream" learn about culture or see themselves in cultural perspective in school any more than do children from language or ethnic minorities. Instead, culture is framed out of view, either as the null curriculum underlying academic learning but never mentioned in relation to it, or as marginal "enrichment" of the curriculum to celebrate ethnic foods and feasts.

Culturalectomy limits all students' learning about themselves and others, a condition that enables the tacit imposition of whitestream culture on successive generations of all of our citizens. The collective identity of Euro-American pupils (and the majority of their teachers) as "White" frames them, not culturally, historically, or economically, or even in terms of gender. Rather, their identity is framed racially—with "whitness" being the normal or unmarked cultural form. As the unmarked form, it seems to require no reflection or exploration. Nor does it flag a system of identity and identification that rests on oppositions, usually between unequals (Richards, 1999). Thus, failure to explore cultural background is obviously a loss for each individual, but it is also a profound loss for a democratic community. Denial of culture in teacher education similarly precludes an historical, contextual analysis that might help us examine how we became the teachers we are—that is, how our histories shape our practices, assumptions, and expectations. When I ask my students to write vignettes of their cultural experience as literacy learners, they are usually nonplussed. "I don't have a story," they say. "I'm not anything." Responses like these lack a sense of history or place. The normal or "unmarked" form is the bland, commonsense one. It is the water the fish would be the last to discover. By that designation, it marks the alternative as, perhaps colorful, but also abnormal, nonmainstream.

Lack of cultural understanding reinforces Euro-American teachers' sense of "us" as normal (mainstream, White, or colorless) and "them" as abnormal (minority, of color, non-native speaking). Yet implicitly, the unmarked form is defined in its relationship to the marked form. To be

---

[2]I am grateful to the participants in a discussion on "Anthropology at the Crossroads" sponsored by the American Educational Studies Association in November 1999, for this insight.

"not anything" is to deny that we are enmeshed in systems in which oppositions are used to define self and other (Frankenberg, 1993; Morrison, 1994). To be non-White in America is to have your history distorted or forgotten in the curriculum. To be White in U.S. schools is to experience a kind of personal, political, and social amnesia. This forgetting makes it impossible to remember one's forebears' experience of being "outside," acknowledge the privileged position one may now occupy, or reflect on how access to this position is gained by some and denied to others. To the extent that European immigrants and their descendants have learned to conflate being "American" with being "White,"[3] they participate, however unwittingly, in the exclusion of non-European immigrants and their descendants from full participation in our national community (Alba, 1990).

Viewed this way, telling and reading of stories of culture is not an educational frill. It is an activity central to identifying the sources of our identities as Americans and, in the process, of identifying the sources of American inequality. Using the history of Italian Americans as an example, Richards (1999) challenges the descendants of other European immigrant groups to "come to terms" with their cultural heritage. What was it, he asks, "in the Italian experience that made emigration to America, despite all its difficulties, even injustices so worthwhile a risk and so acceptable a trade-off for this historically risk-averse people?" (Richards, 1999, p. 9). And, more troubling, what was it that changed immigration from appealing to threatening, such that, having arrived, Italians joined other immigrants in restricting subsequent immigration and imposing racist assumptions and policies on Americans of color (paraphrased from Richards, 1999, p. 9). Answering these questions involves history, memory, and imagination.

Delpit (1995) urges this kind of self-study among White teachers, especially because they serve as gatekeepers to their pupils' participation in the wider society. For this reason, she says, "it is vital that teachers and teacher educators explore their own beliefs and attitudes about non-white and non-middle-class people" (p. 179). Yet many, if not most, teachers believe precisely the opposite. Assuming that it is impolite, even racist, to notice and talk about race, teachers assume they are expected to be "colorblind." The White teacher's neutrality about race or ethnicity is thought to be fair and a part of offering each pupil the same educational

---

[3]Throughout this volume, the terms White, Caucasian, and Euro-American are used to refer to the descendants of European immigrants.

experiences from which to rise or fall on his or her own merit (Ferdman, 1990; Paley, 1979/1989). Thus, teachers work toward achieving on a "level playing field" where all children are treated as if they are the same. Yet to deny racial, linguistic, cultural, and economic background is not to treat all children equally but to retreat from the awareness that differences do make a difference in school, especially as they confer or deny privilege and power.

MacIntyre (1997) observes that denial of difference has "implications for teaching practice—which include such things as the choice of curriculum materials, student expectations, grading procedures, and assessment techniques—just to name a few" (pp. 14–15). Teachers are thus part of the equation, not neutral observers dismissing, with what Morrison (1992) calls the "generous liberal gesture," inequalities in school and society (pp. 9–10). Talk about culture in terms of one's own experience and in dialogue with the personal narratives (both written and spoken) of others can be educative for teachers—not only about the cultural diversity of their pupils, but about their own identities. Such activity can help teachers recognize that although the role they are assuming as "teacher" is a racialized one, the identities of those who teach are not limited to and by the formal role they assume.

Britzman (1986, cited in Johnson, 1997) argues that by seeing teaching as a situated practice within a social and historical context, we can, as teachers, critically identify our "institutional biography" (p. 453) as well as our ongoing, negotiated autobiography as individuals. Greer Johnson, a scholar of teacher education, asserts that discovering the constraints of the teacher role enables us to assess ways we might engage that role. With this insight, we do not disappear into the putative role but can potentially envision a range of choices in how we enact our teacher role as well as in how we choose to identify ourselves (Florio-Ruane, 1989; Goffman, 1961; Johnson, 1997). Johnson further notes that exploring and exploiting differences, especially ones of dissonance, can help teachers learn that, in Britzman's words, "whereas role can be assigned, the taking up of an identity is a constant social negotiation" (Britzman, 1992, cited in Johnson, 1997, pp. 823–824).

## THE WEBS WE WEAVE

Anthropologist Clifford Geertz (1973) describes culture with an evocative metaphor drawn from the writing of Max Weber. Geertz writes that "man is an animal suspended in webs of significance he himself has spun, I take culture to be those webs . . ." (p. 5). This metaphor suggests that culture is both meaning and the process of making meaning. Culture, when thought of as having these characteristics, would clearly be fundamental to the process of education, not a peripheral topic to be trotted out for the annual ethnic festival. Culture as meaning is a human accomplishment, not a trait to be doled out "one to a customer." As both the web and the weaving, we all make local cultural meaning. We also connect the webs of our local microcultures into a much more complex network of webs linking human beings over time and across distance and difference. To that end, multiculturalism is, in Goodenough's (1976) words, "the normal human experience." Given this understanding of culture and multiculturalism, we might approach our teaching with the awareness that it is we, not some abstract group (e.g., "the Navajo") or "other" (e.g., the bilingual child in the third row) who are multicultural. And to study culture is to study human life, not to impose stereotyping categories on individuals or groups.

Like the individually, gorgeous webs spiders weave in mid-summer on my 20th floor apartment windows, cultural study can concern itself with how people make meaning in particular, local contexts. We must also be alert to how those local webs of meaning are networked as human beings make their way through everyday lives and lifetimes. Ultimately, we are not "parallel players" endlessly spinning and repairing our cultural webs, oblivious to and disconnected from the spinners working on the webs a few feet away. Instead, our webs are linked in cultural networks— filaments the radiate from context to context, the latticework we create and navigate as we move from family to school, from peer group to workplace (Anderson-Levitt, 2001). From this point of view, school is not about educating youngsters to leave one web for another, more "mainstream" one. Rather, it is about educating students to be spinners of webs, travelers who are and will be able to make culture as they engage with others in many contexts, and over a lifetime.

Travelers have long been aware that cultural understanding involves making sense of the means by which others make meaning. This may be accomplished quite literally, by traveling to new places or entering microcultures whose practices are unfamiliar. It may also be possible to experience some of the traveler's disorientation and self–other discovery by studying texts people craft to depict their lives. For this reason, autobiography is one genre that is growing in importance for the purpose of cultural study. Reading autobiography cross-culturally, in Proefriedt's (1990) words, the individual becomes radically decentered, geographically and otherwise, and ceases to identify one cultural experience as a set of universal truths against which other lesser claims are measured. Nothing stands at the center. All is in motion. The immigrant, or cultural outsider, is given access to this fundamental truth, at once liberating and frightening, of the modern world. Relatedly, it is the movement between and among cultures, and the recognition of fragmentation within cultures, that leads to a reformulation of the central purposes of education. (p. 78)

Although cultural study of this sort has occurred as long as human beings have traveled (Hymes, 1982), contemporary life is marked by burgeoning and very rapid intercultural contact among many people of the world. In the early 21st century, we are intensely aware of what psychologists Hermans and Kempens (1998) describe as, "the unprecedented character of worldwide interconnectedness that is realized by the increasing impact of new technologies" (p. 1111). Technology speeds up the networking process, expands the networks, and makes it possible for cultural experience rapidly to transcend geography and time.[4] The explosion of intercultural contact in our historical moment challenges us to rethink our social and psychological explanations of learning and development and our vision of literacy and education (The New London Group, 1996). We must teach with the insight that culture is bound up with learning. Both are dynamic and change in interaction with each other. In a metaphor echoing but also expanding on Geertz' "webs," Cole (1996), following Vygotsky, describes learning, viewed in cultural perspective, as a "weaving together" of phylogeny and social history as these "coincide and mingle" during an individual's—and a society's—development (pp. 181–182).

## ONLY CONNECT?

Nowhere is the weaving of culture and development more apparent and important than in the classroom. Teachers need to study the webs they have learned to create and in which they are suspended not only because they may differ from the webs of their students, but also because, as webs, they both support and ensnare. Languages make talk possible by limiting the range of lexical and grammatical choices. Likewise, the shared sys-

---

[4]I am thankful to Chip Bruce for reminding me, however, that this access via technology is limited by political and economic inequalities and, indeed, may rapidly increase the gaps separating people on the basis of wealth.

tems of meaning that make our everyday lives sensible limit our understanding of others' local meaning systems. Our ways of making meaning
locate us, biasing our interpretations of meaning and our understanding of
others. Left unexamined, they can distort our encounters with the diverse
learners in our charge. Yet teachers are among the least likely people to
experience cultural contact as destabilizing of their entering assumptions
or enlightening about their biases. This is the case in part because teachers
work in a profession historically charged with fostering assimilation. It is
also because teachers bear large amounts of power and responsibility for
instructing and evaluating others.

In the teacher role, people are accustomed and expected to have the
"right answers" and to be able to explain why others do not. It is difficult
for teachers to explore the cultural and developmental landscape of their
classrooms with the "dual vision" of the participant-observer. The press
of their workload and the isolation of their role lead teachers to see their
task not as one of engagement in which contact with others is mutually
transformative, but rather, as one of "connecting," meeting learners in
some zone of proximal development in which it is the student who is
expected to change by virtue of this encounter. Yet, as the well-meaning
but naïve Schlegel sisters learned in E.M. Forster's (1921) novel,
*Howard's End*, from which the evocative phrase "only connect" comes,
much harm can be done by powerful people meddling, in the name of
"connecting," with the lives of less powerful people. Like teachers in our
time, educated young women of privilege living in England at the turn of
last century were faced with a growing sense that their isolated dominion
was fading. Their lives were, for better and for worse, increasingly complicated by the diverse mix of people from various backgrounds, nationalities, and social positions claiming England as their home. And so they
saw their task—and their opportunity—to venture into connection with
others different from themselves and threatening to their sense of order
by virtue of their differences in ethnicity, language, or social station. The
extent to which that connection across such differences can be a life-
enhancing, authentic two-way street of risk and engagement, is a theme
of Forster's work in the post-Victorian age. It is also a theme of our work
at the turn of a new century.

Connection is inauthentic when a teacher (or other powerful person),
however well intentioned, does not risk personal engagement and the possibility of transformation by means of engagement with her pupils (or
other persons in subordinate or dependent positions). Although this is
surely the case in a variety of relationships, it seems central to that of

teacher and pupil(s). The educational relationship is, at its essence, not a one-way street. In fact, it is a complex encounter in which more and less experienced people are changed in and through their engagement not only with one another, but also with the subject matter of their transaction. In this way, culture is expressed, created, and transformed as individuals' grow in understanding. The process is one of development, not one of indoctrination.

Ideally, then, education is the encounter and transformation of, in Hawkins' (1974) words, "I, Thou, and It." Yet, routine practice often strays far from this kind of engagement and shared risk. Particularly as we transact across difference in ethnicity, age, income, first language, social class, and the like, the chance that the teacher's relationship to the learners will default to an inauthentic, one-way connection is great. The example on page 31 is drawn from my own recent experience and illustrates.

Cross-cultural experience should unsettle and transform us. Sometimes the process involves loss, sometimes it yields change; it invariably involves risk and requires engagement. To learn about ourselves as we try to learn about others does not mean that we assume a stance of bland or "nihilistic" cultural relativism. Rather, Geertz (1983) argues that we learn about others and ourselves by taking our own values into account and critically examining them as we try to understand the unfamiliar. In so doing, Geertz says, "one welds the processes of self-knowledge, self-perception, self-understanding to those of other-knowledge, other-perception, other understanding" (pp. 181–182). In this sense, learning about culture is always and profoundly autobiographical. In the example, to enter a pedagogical relationship with learners, my interns and I needed to confront the limits of our knowledge about mathematics instruction as well as our stereotypes and the diminished expectations to which they give rise. We also learned that we were, paraphrasing Kailin (1998), "unconscious of and indeed socialized not to think about" our participation in the structures that support and maintain educational inequalities on the basis of race (p. 83). How might we learn to see culture in our lives and those of our students in a more thoughtful way?

In many instances, the isolation and insulation of our sites of practice in teacher education make it difficult for teachers (both beginning and experienced) to have the experience of epoque, that breaking of ordinary frames for understanding, that is so common in travel and in the anthropologists' fieldwork. Greene (1994) urges as an alternative that teachers study the literature of many diverse lives in order to "break out of the confinement of monologism, open themselves to pluralism, become aware of

## Susan's Story

Several years ago, I took on a new and challenging assignment mentoring several interns in an inner-city school. Nearly all of the interns' pupils were African American and lived in low-income households. Although the interns were working in different grades and classrooms, all were observing students' difficulty moving from understanding a concept concretely (i.e., with "manipulatives" such as M&Ms and paper strips) to expressing that concept abstractly (i.e., in words and numbers). The interns and I suffered limited knowledge of teaching math and precious little experience working with children in this urban school context. With the best of intentions, we constructed an account of the children's difficulties resting on poverty. We cited the lack of books in their homes, the need for parents to work multiple jobs and therefore be less than participatory in pupils' school lives, and the lack of a variety of opportunities to practice outside of the classroom what we hoped they would learn inside the classroom. In linking poverty, and by extension, race, to learning mathematics, we were making efforts to understand or connect with pupils. Trying out our "poverty" explanation on the professor teaching math methods, he shook his head wearily. Having read the interns' lesson plans and heard their reports, he remarked that a more obvious and likely reason for the children's difficulties might be that we had, in fact, neglected to guide, model, or otherwise instruct them in making the sought after transfer from manipulatives to text. We had not taught what we hoped they would learn. Firmly he said, "Rich or poor, White or Black—learning to think mathematically is hard. That is why we need teachers."

more possible ways of being and of attending to the world" (p. 21). In reading our own lives, we link past and future; in reading the lives of other narrators, we, in Greene's words "lend them our lives." In consequence,

> The materials of the readers' experience . . . cannot but be ordered . . . in unfamiliar ways . . . readers see dimensions of that experience that are ordinarily

invisible, hear aspects of it ordinarily lost in silence. Not only may there be a
pull toward communitas . . . readers may be moved to new modes of self-defini-
tion in their very awareness of difference. . . . (p. 22)

By telling my story and reading or hearing another's, I am a stranger
negotiating meaning among strangers. I find some points of potential contact; make mistakes or miscues; become more aware of my prior knowledge and its limits; construct new understandings. I recognize my own
understandings not as "natural" or "normal," but as culturally made. This
experience is unsettling for teachers who expect (and are expected) to
know the point of a story before teaching it, the point of a situation before
engaging it; the route of an activity before it is traveled. Literature educator Reed Dasenbrock (1992) urges teachers, like anthropologists, to adopt
a model of learning as "interpretation" rather than "possession." He
encourages us to think unconventionally of our reading, writing, and
speaking, not as "the demonstration of knowledge already in place, but as
a scene of learning" (p. 39).

# CHAPTER 3

# The Stories
# by Which We Teach

The absence of a narrative study of culture in teacher education does not mean that we approach teaching absent stories of culture. Instead, we tacitly hold stories of culture that organize what we see, do, and think in the name of public education. Writing about classroom discourse, Cazden (1986) describes a "default" mode in teaching. She observes that, like the default settings in her computer that maintain the characteristics of her text, classroom talk is patterned in ways that reproduce the characteristics of oral texts for learning. Teachers ask questions, students respond, teachers evaluate. Questions tend to be testlike, assessing rather than inquiring, and so forth. Each time we turn on the computer the default settings operate—unless we take direct, explicit steps to change them. Likewise, Cazden argues that direct effort is needed to alter the automatic patterns of our teaching so that classroom interactions and the learning possible within them might be changed.

By analogy, we can think of teacher education as having a default mode for teachers' understanding of culture. Culture is what "other people" (usually different from us in skin color, first language, or economic circumstance) "have." As such, culture is thought of as a trait of a group of people and typically operates to limit opportunity, prompt conflict, or otherwise isolate. Schooling is intended to level across cultural differences, at best rendering them irrelevant to students' learning, educational advancement, and employability. Because teachers and teacher educators are enmeshed in a web of shared knowledge, relationships, and practices sustaining this status quo, teacher education tends to be a weak intervention into teachers' default beliefs about diversity (Zeichner, 1993). Pre- and in-service curricula tend to reinforce stereotypes, especially when lectures and textbooks are the sole or primary ways we learn about culture (Duesterberg, 1998). In addition, field experiences, even when they introduce beginners to diverse pupils, rarely offer chances for them to learn from teachers working "against the grain" (Cochran-Smith, 1991) of the profession's color and culture "blindness." Even teacher education's contemporary focus on reflection tends to strengthen cultural biases if it is not undertaken critically (Dressman, 1998). Yet as in classroom discourse, it is possible to change the talk and texts of our practice to cultivate engagement and more complex learning. Let's look first, however, at the default mode to which our practice tends.

## THE "DEFAULT MODE" IN OUR THINKING ABOUT CULTURE

Beginning teachers characteristically embrace two explanations for the learning difficulties of diverse pupils (Paine, 1990). One cites the child's intrinsic psychological characteristics determining what is possible to for the child to learn (e.g., "Adam can't read because he is learning disabled."). The second is a cultural explanation where responsibility for learning difficulties rests with the family's childrearing practices that are thought to be culturally determined (e.g., "Eve could learn to read if only here parents were more involved in her schooling."). In each case, the learner's difficulties lie mostly outside the teacher's sphere of influence. Given by the student's biography and/or by the hard wiring of his or her nervous system, the story has already been written. The cultural explanation is typically invoked as we attempt to understand the educational difficulties of pupils from racial, ethnic, and language minority backgrounds. Thus, a limited understanding of culture on the teacher's part is a limiting factor when he or she interprets the school performance of diverse youngsters (Grant, 1989; Trueba, 1989). When youngsters exhibit differences in communication style in school, a teacher's default mode of thinking tends toward the following deficit view:

1. Cultural differences are problems rather than resources for learning.
2. Pupil performance is the result of the two primary factors of pupil psychology and family socialization.
3. Cultural background is largely determinant of school achievement and future socioeconomic standing.

This interpretation of culture is reflected in the comments of two members of the Future Teachers' Autobiography Club. Placed as student teachers in the nearby state capital, they soon found themselves working not only in a new role, but in classroom environments different from the suburban and rural ones to which they had been accustomed. Sometimes, they unburdened as part of the book club's conversations. Conditions in their schools were, indeed, different from conditions in the more affluent, suburban settings where their peers taught and where they had gone to school. There were fewer resources of time and materials available to teachers. Class size was large, much greater than in the suburban schools, and programs such as art, music, and physical education had been reduced or eliminated to focus limited economic resources in the district on the basic skills. These meant that teachers had less time to plan and were obligated to supervise even recess and lunch. Yet because the district's standardized test scores were relatively low, teachers felt pressed to teach more and also more effectively. With little room in such a stressful environment for teachers or students to stretch—emotionally or physically, it is not surprising that conflict among students and between teachers and students was common. Complicating matters, the school counselor had a very large caseload and, due to budget cuts, worked in multiple schools across the city. Many parents worked multiple jobs or lacked cars, so it was difficult for them to visit the school, even on parents' night. Some did not have telephones, and many were transient, moving in and out of relatives' homes or staying one step ahead of the landlord when economic times were especially difficult. Thus, communication between teacher and family was difficult and spotty.

These realities of political, social, and economic context do not in themselves account for or explain why some children are successful in school and others are not. But they are factors complicating and stressing the educational experience and possibilities of teachers, youngsters, and families alike. It is interesting, however, that in their "kernel narratives" (Kalcik, 1975), the student teachers do not refer to these constraints and stresses. Instead, teacher efficacy, to the extent that it exists, is at the individual level—the one-on-one dynamics of "he said, she said." One told us the following:

> I was almost in tears this past week because kids were so disrespectful to me. I was almost in tears. I thought, How dare you treat me that way, especially when . . . the one child, he was really terrible to me. Disrespectful, kicking desks, hitting his desk, just going out of control. I had bent over backwards to be kind and respectful toward him, and when I respected him and was so kind toward him, I took it as such an attack that he was like that to me . . .

As she trailed off, the other young teacher working in the city added the following:

> And their cut-downs, I mean, my kids, I wouldn't think of some of the things they say. They are . . . they get it at home or something, but they are beyond my level of thinking for cutdowns. (Meeting Transcript, 3/25/93)

When we take a close look at these kernel narratives, we see evidence of the default mode and of the difficult position in which it places teachers, youngsters, and families. Although each teacher spoke poignantly and with great emotion about problems in the behavior, motivation, or formative experiences of her pupils, she framed the classroom's problems in personal terms. Lone rangers in showdowns with youngster whom they had expected to be respectful and compliant, the teachers were hurt ("How could he do this to me?"), bemused ("I respected him and was so kind toward him."), even fearful ("I took it as such an attack."). One found an explanation in the family's childrearing practices ("They get it at home or something."). Both seemed pressed to closure, thus turning a complex problem of practice into one they could not solve but might dismiss by judging students and families. Ironically, by locating agency exclusively in the teacher ("I bent over backwards."), the student ("How dare he?"), and the parent ("They get it at home or something."), the narratives actually close off possible routes for inquiry and action. Overdrawing the characters (the teacher, child, and family), the story lines lack exploration of complexity in characters' experience. It is hard to see how their encounters, however difficult, "make sense." Because the vignettes are not situated historically, socially, economically, culturally, or politically, the resources for interpretation available within them are very limited. Moreover, the characters are placed in opposition despite their shared embeddedness in institutions where they have few resources and little power is not part of the story.

These kernel narratives are not factual accounts. They are performances within conversation and, as such, present "what happened" figuratively and in ways reflecting and reinforcing the narrator's common-sense and presentation of self (Bauman, 1986). As "constructed dialogues" they do not directly quote, but rather "report" who said what to whom. They are, in Tannen's (1989) words, "primarily the creation of the speaker rather than the party quoted" (p. 99). This is an important feature of narratives that we tell, hear, or read about practice. As "constructions," they can be reconstructed to try out other renditions of "who we (and they) are, and what we (and they) are doing." If the story were retold in these terms it would, perhaps, be no less "true" or "false." But it likely would offer a different problem, complicating action, or denouement. What can teachers do to frame and solve problems of their practice within complex institutions and their bureaucracies? What are my professional goals and responsibilities in this setting? Why am I afraid of or apt to hold low expectations for students and families racially, ethnically, linguistically, or economically different from me? Must I work in isolation from my colleagues or are there ways for us to join forces to enhance the climate for learning in our school? What stirs resistance in my youngsters' experience of school? Who are their families? What are their hopes and expectations for their children's education? In Moll and Greenberg's (1990) terms, what untapped "funds of knowledge" do families hold and how might my colleagues and I reach out to create "zones of possibility" or new contexts and activities for learning with them?

## DURABLE NARRATIVES IN EDUCATION

The purpose of this example is not to judge the student teachers. It is, rather, to illustrate how the images and narratives we hold, unexamined, penetrate our thinking and, indeed, come to be our experience. And, in point of fact, these young teachers are far from alone in making such attributions and interpretations about minority and economically disadvantaged children and adults. Leacock (1971) critiqued the application of a cultural explanation to the experiences of the poor as yet another way to label people. She lamented the fact that although culture might illuminate local meaning and help us to understand human diversity, it was often applied in social science and policy as one more determinist system to sort and separate people into unequal groups. Following Leacock's critique of the concept of a "culture of poverty," another anthropologist, Micaela di Leonardo, notes that social scientists have tended to make the following deficit assumptions as they theorize about culture and ethnic identity. These assumptions mirror what educational researchers identify as entering beliefs of teachers:

1.  Cultures are unique, bounded groups–often standing in conflict with one another;

2.  Culture is passed on essentially intact from generation to generation within families;

3.  Immigrants and subsequent generations of their offspring have in common a static stock of cultural knowledge and practices usually referred to as ethnicity;

4.  The worth or value of cultural knowledge and practices is measured by the economic success of the ethnic group holding them;

5.  When ethnic groups fail to thrive economically, that failure is explainable in terms of the inadequacies of their culture, especially its family and childrearing practices. (paraphrased and adapted from di Leonardo, 1984)

Differences in language, race, ethnicity, and social class are seen as explanatory of school failure and, as such, are problems rather than resources. The divide between home and school is wide, especially difficult to bridge when the child's parents are non-middle class, ethnically or linguistically diverse, or have few years of schooling. In a painful double bind, the student must become alienated from home and background to succeed in school. Tragically, her or his family must actively support such alienation if school success is to be possible. This idea was expressed by Richard Rodriguez, who adapted Hoggart's image of the "scholarship boy" to think about his own life in the autobiography, *Hunger of Memory*:

> The scholarship boy must move between environments, his home and the classroom, which are at cultural extremes, opposed. With his family, the boy has the intense pleasure of intimacy, the family's consolation in feeling public alienation. Lavish emotions texture home life. *Then*, at school, the instruction bids him to trust lonely reason primarily. Immediate needs set the pace of his parents' lives. From his mother and father the boy learns to trust spontaneity and nonrational ways of knowing. *Then*, at school, there is mental calm. Teachers emphasize the value of a reflectiveness that opens a space between thinking and immediate action. (Rodriguez, 1982, p. 46)

Literary critics call narrative devices like the scholarship boy *tropes*. From the Greek word meaning, "to twist," a trope is a figurative use of language that turns experience in a particular way and for a particular effect (Lentriccia & McLaughlin, 1990). Like their cousins, metaphors, tropes are yarns we spin to make a fabric of lived experience. Put bluntly, in Didion's (1979) words, "We tell ourselves stories in order to live . . . we look for the sermon in the suicide, the moral lesson in the murder of five. We interpret what we see . . . we live entirely by the imposition of a narrative line upon disparate images . . . or at least we do for awhile" (Didion, 1979, p. 11). "For awhile" is a phrase worth contemplating. We can and should ask why these stories work and for whom, as well as why and how these story lines fail to work. So deeply a part of our collective consciousness, our stories assume the force of truth, and we lose awareness of them as social and linguistic constructions. In short, they come to shape our experience (Emihovich, 1995; Lakoff & Johnson, 1980). Thus, a good portion of our education as teachers takes place within the inheritance of such stories, at least until they either fail us or we are invited to stand outside them and consider them critically (Gee, 1989).

In our thinking about U.S. education, the story of the scholarship boy explains diverse youngsters' school difficulties. Many versions of this yarn have been spun in research and in the "common sense" of educational practice (Florio-Ruane & McVee, 2000). The lonely child crossing the border from home to school touches all of us, because any life presents times of difficult transition. It levels across a wide range of experiences of loss and change (Cohen, 1976). Most teachers can embrace it easily and without examining inequality. Readable as both "us" and "them, " this image appears in status quo educational discourse (e.g., the kindergarten "round up" or the assessment of youngsters' school "readiness") and also appears in reforms intended to assist diverse youngsters' entry into the school environment (e.g., "inclusion"). In Kailin's (1998) words, it "look(s) at the world from the top down" (p. 81). An omniscient narrator describes the movement of the student between separate, unquestioned worlds. Thus, the image of the scholarship boy reinforces our assumptions about school even as we aim to make school more "accessible." Like the bed of Procrustus, which occupants were stretched or cut to fit, school is entered, not made, by its occupants, and it is students who must be changed to fit.[1]

---

[1]Frederick Erickson helpfully linked this myth to thinking about educational reform.

Other narratives are possible, ones that view the experience of going to school from other perspectives and stances. In some narratives, the border presumed in the scholarship boy's experience is permeable and shifting, and along with it, so is the boy's sense of self in the world. In his second book, *Days of Obligation: An Argument with My Mexican Father*, Rodriguez (1992) tackles this challenge. Published later, it is a complex narrative design, criss-crossing many geographical and personal borders. This book offers a variegated picture of the author's coming of age. More difficult to read and discuss, it breaks the frame of our profession's default mode for thinking about culture and identity. It illustrates the possibility that the "self" is neither static nor one dimensional. It illustrates the possibility that one's autobiography can be revised as the story of self can be told and retold in different ways and for different purposes.[2] And it provides a chance for one to read about a person's life intertextually. I return later in this book to intertextual readings of culture by means of extended contact with diverse autobiographies. With increased experience of difference and contact with diverse interlocutors, the telling of new stories and/or retelling familiar ones in more nuanced and complex ways is possible.

In research on the cultural stories of beginning teachers, McVee (1999) found that, lacking such opportunities to explore culture reflexively, they used schematic "grand narratives" (also called master or meta narratives in her work). According to McVee, "these are typically compressed or partial narratives that are widely accepted by members of a group. They shape other narratives told within the group, reinforcing members' sense of self, ways of seeing others, and sense of the world" (p. 127). As such, they are part of a person's "primary discourse" (Gee, 1989), or acquired perspective of a social group that has been formative for that person and about which, without experiences in other discourses or communities and practices, the person is uncritical. In McVee's research, as in research others have conducted on learning to teach (Denyer & Florio-Ruane, 1995), the teacher candidate's primary discourse accompanies him or her into his or her university classes and field experiences. It is only by means of explicit educational interventions that the beginning teacher's "default mode"(Cazden, 1986) for thinking about teaching and learners may be changed.

Grand or meta narratives are socially constructed. They gloss complexity by weaving information in ways that make particular shared inter-

---

[2] I thank Enrique Trueba for this insight.

pretations possible. They tend to be embraced for and by members of an interpretive community (Fish, 1980), serving and reinforcing the beliefs, values, and interests of that community. When we read *Hunger of Memory* in the Future Teachers Autobiography Club, the "scholarship boy" had immediate appeal. As was common in our conversations, one participant voiced a response to this trope by echoing it in her own words and in terms of her own experiences. As such, she was making a move toward engagement with Rodriguez as a speaker, bringing him discursively to our table. Here is what she said about the scholarship boy to the assenting nods of the rest of us at the table:

> I talk to my dad about this. I am thinking, what if you are an inner-city Detroit 16-year-old Black male and you want to succeed, want to learn, want to succeed in education to get out of poverty. I guess that is a kind of common thing, but it kind of hit me like a lightening bolt. If I choose one thing that I want, I'm going to be hurt. If I choose the other thing that I want to be—I want to be intimate, I want to live like I have always lived, to enjoy my culture and the things I like in life, I won't have this. It is one or the other. You are isolated. (Meeting Transcript, 3/25/93)

Like many of the beginners' stories analyzed by McVee, this one is schematic. It holds tight to an available story line but is neither nuanced nor detailed. Yet among the listeners, who similarly lack knowledge or experience of the situation Marcia describes, the account is received uncritically. With a collective sigh, our group moves on, relieved to have made this narrative connection to the lonely Latino boy and the alienated African-American teenager.

Marcia's telling of the experience of boys from Detroit need not be valid in order to be taken as explanatory by members of the book club. It echoes Rodriguez's account of the "scholarship boy" and evokes connections with other book club members' experiences of change and loss. As such, the story has face validity. In the absence of broader and deeper knowledge of the subject, the story suffices. McVee (1999) points out that stories like this one are, "deeply sedimented within culture and serve to sustain cultural understanding as tacit and shared. As such they are very powerful but they are also very limited in their form, scope, and evaluation and limiting in the ways that they construct and constrain an individual's cultural identity" (p. 154).

McVee's research finds that when a topic arises about which teacher candidates hold wider and deeper knowledge and experience, master narratives tend to be critiqued in conversation as incomplete or incorrect.

Sometimes they are rejected all together as participants tell stories explicitly counter to prevailing cultural stories. In these cases, stories tend to be more detailed and complex and, as such, are open to multiple and varied readings. This occurs, for example, when McVee's students discuss Amy Tan's (1991) autobiographical novel, *The Kitchen God's Wife*. An important theme raised in the novel is that of spousal abuse. The members of McVee's class discuss it with vigor, ardency, and controversy. The discussion stands in contrast to sketchy, unexamined narratives told about another, far less familiar topic, the school experiences of young African-American males, arising out of one student's description of an in-service workshop titled, "The Black Child Placed in Crisis." The participants in the conversations McVee studied had more direct experience of spousal abuse. One worked in a shelter for battered women. Others, as young females of marriageable age, read, talked, and thought a good deal about the topic. Knowledge, in short, enriched the teacher candidates' traversal of the topic and with that the number, complexity, and critique of stories told in conversation about it (McVee, 1999).

## RETHINKING STORIES OF CULTURE
## FOR TEACHER EDUCATION

As much as it involves ethnic food, costume, or holiday practices, learning about culture also involves exploration of subtler aspects of life not typically noted for comment. These include nuances in the styles by which we express ourselves in verbal and nonverbal behavior, family stories echoing across people and generations, and fleeting images of our upbringing in families, neighborhoods, churches, and peer groups. This material is fodder for literary representations of cultural identity. It dominates coming-of-age narratives as well as immigrant stories of the disorienting and reorienting of self that accompanies movement from one place to another. Ironically, however, this is precisely the material framed out of view in academic descriptions of culture.

Students of education are rarely taught about culture in terms of searching, evocative questions and themes. Like the classrooms in which they will teach, their university classes in education are not known, in Harold Rosen's (1985) terms, for their "nurture of narrative" nor are they characterized by conversation and personal narrative among students. Instead, we teach about teaching—its foundational knowledge and its practices—in decidedly expository ways. Here, culture is represented as a static system of knowledge organizing the practices and interpretive frames of a group of people—their idealized "ways of life." This kind of generalized description (e.g., "the Navajo way of life") inevitably stereotypes.[3] It wrings from culture and from individual lives the unique, the particular, the conflictual, and the contradictory. While done in the spirit of rigorous theorizing about human nature, the rhetorical shift from participant to distanced observer and describer inevitably changes our perspective and hence our text (Pratt, 1986).

McDiarmid and Price (1990) studied an in-service curriculum on cultural diversity based on such expository texts and contexts. They found that both the texts and the means by which they were used to transmit information to teachers about culture encouraged rather than diminished teachers' inclinations to stereotype youngsters on the basis of ethnic and cultural backgrounds. The observer's written report of the field experience as "research" can leave out the detail as well as the drama of the informants' lived experience and also neglect the role of the fieldwork in transforming the researcher's understanding of self and other (Salvio, 1990). Such texts neglect the narrative dimensions of cultural experience and description. Relying on them to learn about culture, teachers are apt to sees others' lives as frozen or lifeless and their own as aloof from cultural forces shaping identity and life chances. This is particularly troublesome in the preparation of literacy educators because language (both oral and written) is intimately tied to culture. If our understanding of cultural practice is frozen, our understanding of language and literacy development will be as well.

Culture, as a static state or system, is not very interesting to teachers. It is rarely integrated with study of children's development. Nor is it studied within the history of schools, conceptions of school improvement and change, or the dynamics of classroom instruction. Finally, culture is not studied as central to the process of language and literacy learning. Instead, culture is often taken out of context, pushed to the margins in a course or two on the foundations of education, typically just prior to or on completion of the methods courses and field experiences. One course is but a small portion of the total curriculum for learning to teach and is, ironically, tightly "bordered" so as tacitly to convey that culture is outside the

---

[3]There are times when it is purposeful for people to use such stereotypes to advance, for example, civil rights of a group. But such uses should not be confused with arguing that a generalized picture of a group of people is tantamount to understanding culture or individual experience within that group (Donna Dehyle, personal communication, November 1999).

major work of teaching or learning to teach (Boyle-Baise, 1997). Moreover, "foundation" is an ambiguous metaphor—it is both the underlying strength and structure of a building and also its cellar. Like cellars, literacy teachers often experience the foundation curriculum as dark, musty, and easily ignored as we tend to our busy lives "upstairs." Marginalized this way, culture is not a meaningful, coherent part of what literacy teachers need to understand in order to teach well.

In order to create a profession more reflective of the strengths of our population's history and diversity, we need to transform the texts and contexts of teachers' learning to include multiple voices and stories of culture, literacy, and education. Gazing both inward and outward, and in dialogue with others, we might thus uncover culture not as trait by which to label others, but as a shared human experience of making meaning. Such a process would take, in McHenry's (1997) words, "a conscious step away from the position of contemplation or observation (of) the student (as) 'separated object'" (p. 349). This change in the curriculum for teacher education would entail a shift of culture from peripheral to central in teachers' thinking about literacy and learning. In so doing, culture would not be defined in its default mode. Rather, its meanings would be open to inquiry and discovery. Meier calls this, "the kind of mental paradigm shift, the 'aha' that is at the heart of learning, [and that] usually requires more than being told by an authority or shown a demonstration" (Meier, 1995, cited in McHenry, 1997, p. 349).

Vivian Paley exemplifies this kind of "aha" at the heart of learning in *White Teacher*, the autobiography with which this book began. In terms of its design, the book can be thought of as linked vignettes, each undermining of the young teacher's entering beliefs and knowledge, about herself and her students. One example encapsulates this process of the author's identifying and rethinking her story. Paley discovers that she not only holds higher expectations for White students than for Black students,[4] but also that she privileges more affluent students over those from low income families. This discovery begins with the breakdown of Paley's narrative. She inadvertently learns that one of her struggling, low-income Black students, Kathy, has a high-achieving older sister in another classroom. Paley considers her low expectations of Kathy, wondering what she might be missing. To get to know Kathy better, Paley decides to listen and watch her interactions more closely and to engage her in longer strips of conversation. As she observes and talks with Kathy and her friend, Charlene, she notices that the girls speak in Black English Vernacular. Paley (1979/1989) quotes from transcript of audiotapes of their overheard talk:

Leave me be girl. You ain't my friend no more.

If I tells my mamma, she gonna whip your tail.

My mama never whip me, girl. (p. 28)

On hearing them, Paley admits, "I was amused by this frequent banter between them. But it was not *my* language. This was not the language of children from educated families, who live on educated streets and have educated conversations at home" (p. 28). As she talks with Kathy and Charlene, she observes the girls gradually coming to shift in speech style from Black English Vernacular to what Paley calls, "middle class school speech." She also realizes that the students from more affluent, educated households make this shift more often and with ease. Paley describes her "aha" as follows:

> I began to realize that many of the black children regularly used different speech patterns when playing with each other and when playing with white children or teachers. They moved in and out of this speech with ease. They had no problems here. *I* had the problem. Actually, I made the same sort of instant transformation with certain Jewish friends. The Yiddish expressions would appear, the inflections, the broken English of the immigrant, all of which resulted in good feelings and frequent laughter. (pp. 28–29)

Paley recollects that not all her Jewish friends received so much pleasure from using Yiddish. She admits that even she, who enjoys the cadence and comfort of Yiddish among Jewish family and friends was, like some of her Black students, reluctant to use a private way of speaking it in a public setting such as school. She considers that although some of her Black students are comfortable using both vernacular and school-appropriate speech styles in her classroom, others from more affluent and educated families may be carefully avoiding using ethnic speech styles "in front of a White teacher." She connects the sense her own students are making to her own experience noting,

> As a child, I would never have wished to draw attention to my differences before a non-Jewish teacher. It may seem that I am overdoing my comparison of Jewish feelings and black feelings. But I am talking about feeling different. Perhaps

---

[4]Because Paley's (1979/1989) book uses the terms *Black* and *White* I have done likewise when paraphrasing or referring to it.

coming to terms with one kind of difference prepares a person for all kinds of differences. At least this is the way it was for me. (Paley, 1979/1989, p. 29)

This insight involves not only Paley's observation of her interactions with Kathy, but also her exercise of what anthropologist, Fischer (1986), calls "the arts of memory" (p. 194). Early in her book, Paley remembers feeling like an outsider when she was a pupil, despite her mother's repeated insistence that she need not feel this way because there were many other Jewish youngsters in her class and school.

Contrasting public and private, Paley does not speak of "minority–majority" distinctions so much as feelings of being an "insider" or an "outsider" to a social system. She, therefore, is able to focus our attention on the effects that racial and ethnic prejudices might have on an individual speaker's choices for how to express herself in a public, institutional setting. When Paley adopts a stance of inquiry toward her own and others' lives, she realizes that there is no particular vice or virtue associated with shifting speech styles or preferring not to. Yet, although speech style is not an index of students' potential to learn, there are profound consequences for what the teacher makes of the speech behaviors of her students. Paley uncovers the possibility that what she calls her "prejudice" is not only racial, but social and economic. And, from this insight, she identifies her own complicity, by virtue of her lowered expectations, in the perpetuation of inequality on the basis of both race and social class.

## LEARNING FROM PALEY'S STORY

Paley's insight does not linger on guilt. As a practitioner, the insight feeds back on her thought and action in the classroom. She reasons from retelling the story of Kathy that it is inappropriate and potentially damaging to equate students' preferences for style shifting to their ability to learn in school. Paley learns, and teaches us by her narrative, that the issue of difference—and how both pupils and teachers come to terms with it—lies at the heart of her teaching problem. Discovering that, like Kathy, she is also subject to feeling different and making decisions about how to speak on that basis, Paley makes a connection with Kathy that is new and educationally generative.

A story within a story, Paley subjects her rendition of Kathy to inquiry and criticism. The drama in this vignette thus turns, not on

Kathy's trouble with learning, but on the teacher's investigation of her own problem. Had Paley not left her classroom and learned about Kathy's sister, the problem would not have arisen. Few factors inside a classroom directly confront the stories that teachers tell themselves about their pupils. Paley also would not have devised a new story unless she had returned her attention to Kathy, this time with the assumption of Kathy's competence and sense making. Nor would it have been possible to tell a different story had Paley not looked at her own life, exercising in particular the artful act of remembering. Such remembering is not recalling forgotten information but making new interpretations by reconstructing past experience. Paley might expect that her experience as a Jewish child might sensitize her to racial prejudice. But she might not have been aware that this experience did not immunize her from prejudice toward others, especially on the basis of race. Moreover, revisiting her past uncovers the root of another prejudice, that her economically and educationally privileged social background biases her to higher expectations from similarly privileged learners, Black and White.

Paley raises difficult issues of racial, ethnic, and social class bias in the modest form of a teaching experience retold. This makes a good story, and perhaps reveals what good stories can do for learning. In Galda's (1998) words, good literature offers us both "mirror and windows." Paley's writing challenges a tendency in both social science and teacher education to place others at a distance in order to understand them—an act that ironically alienates us from both their experiences and our own. According to Cazden and Mehan (1989), this practice conveys to teachers that we have understood others simply because we have talked about them. They quote Landes (1965) in this regard, who warns that

> Heavy use of this prime tool can fail educators in their goal of attuning instruction to actual processes of learning. This happens when educators talk more about pupils than with them and their families. Separateness from the objects of discussion forfeits the experiences words should mirror. (Landes, 1965, p. 64, cited in Cazden & Mehan, 1989)

Teachers face a dizzying array of differences among their pupils. Cazden and Mehan argued that it is more appropriate and important for teachers to adopt an inquiring stance toward the cultural experience of their students than to study lists of characteristics of ethnic groups (Cazden & Mehan, 1989, p. 55). Like Paley's vignette, this seems at first blush to be a simple task. But as it requires surfacing and revising our stories, this is a tall order for teacher education, stretching our thinking not only about culture, but also about the complex learning that is involved in becoming a teacher.

Following Wittgenstein (1953), psychologist Rand Spiro and his associates have described this kind of complex learning with the metaphor of the "criss-cross landscape." They theorize that people learn complex concepts and practices not as simple, linear content mastered once and for all and to be applied in new settings, but flexibly and by repeated examination of rich cases. Learning of complex ideas and practices involves, in Spiro et al.'s words, "a nonlinear traversal of complex subject matter, returning to the same place in the conceptual landscape on different occasions coming from different directions" (Spiro, Feltovich, Jacobson, & Coulson, 1993/1995, p. 10). It is transformative in that it forces prior, tacit knowledge into the light and changes its nature and content as new cases are encountered. This kind of learning prepares us to solve new problems. Because flexibility is key to understanding complexity, it is important, in Spiro and Jehng's (1990) words to "use *multiple representations* for advanced knowledge acquisition in ill-structured domains" (p. 175). In this way, a learner investigates two kinds of complexity: (a) each case has sufficient resonance to enable multiple re-readings or revisiting to access the knowledge it represents; (b) the multiple cases are overlapping, not a set of subtypes of a word's meaning, but instances of a concept "in use."

Culture, as one such complex concept, can and should be studied by teachers in the ill-structured domain of their practice and in forms of teacher education that foster autobiographical inquiry and conversation. It is important for the curriculum of teacher education to prompt examination of diverse narratives of culture—not only canonical ones, but less likely ones, some more distant, others so close to home as to go unnoticed. In this way, teachers might continuously explore culture as a fundamental part of honing their craft and realize that telling stories is a powerful way to understand our lives. However, the stories we tell are limited constructions that should be taken as provisional, works in progress whose problems, complicating action, and resolution should be visited and revisited—as should the nature of our own position as author and, often, protagonist. This idea radically alters our assumptions about how best to learn about culture for the purpose of teaching. And it greatly expands the range of images, activities, settings, and genres by which that learning might occur.

# CHAPTER 4

# Conversation and Narrative in the Future Teachers' Autobiography Club

Learning to teach multiculturally is not reducible to a simple set of techniques, procedures, or homilies. Rather, in Chavez Chavez and O'Donnell's (1998) words, multicultural teaching and learning is "idiosyncratic to the contextual *and* processual experiences the teacher and the learner bring *at the moment of engagement*" (p. 13). To learn about culture I conjectured that beginning teachers would need to experience engagement in an activity that was immediate, compelling, and authentic to their experience and purposes. I thought that such exploration might be fostered in what Haroutunian-Gordon (1998) calls, "interpretive discussion."

This kind of discussion, Haroutunian-Gordon (1991) argues, supports the kind of reflective thinking she elsewhere describes in Socratic terms as a "turning of the soul." Such thinking is sustained in dialogue and follows a pattern wherein participants are able freely and deeply to explore a text. This can, indeed, happen with the guidance of a teacher, but it is primarily actualized in the discourse of the learners. Rather than follow a preordained plan, speakers can recycle or elaborate a sequence of ideas. In talking about a text, they can also choose to follow some ideas and not others in order to "illuminate its meaning for those participating" (Haroutunian-Gordon, 1998, p. 58). In this way, interpretive discussion supports readings, reasoning, and reflection and is central to creating and sustaining an interpretive community.

In 1993, when I founded the Future Teachers' Autobiography Club, I wanted to create an activity and a setting for such engagement. For each of the club's 6 months, the six student teachers joined me at my home for dinner and discussion of a published autobiography. I recruited the participants from the Learning Community, a small, alternative teacher education program I directed at the time and had helped design. I invited student teachers curious about the idea of culture and willing to spend some of their precious student teaching time reading and talking about literature with peers. Although I had never been their instructor, I identified them from suggestions from other program faculty. These students were identified because they seemed to their instructors especially interested in learning more about culture and literacy.

## ABOUT THE CLUB

The Future Teachers' Autobiography Club had no formal agenda. Participants were asked only to commit to coming to the meetings and reading the six books, which I purchased from a small seed grant for each member. I also gave each member a "sketchbook" in which to write notes based on the readings and conversations. I asked permission to read those sketchbooks and also interviewed each club member in the spring after we had completed all of our meetings.

### About My Role

As its founder, host, and participant-observer, I influenced the group considerably. However, I made some decisions intended to shift my role from one of a professor leading a seminar to a member of a book club. First, I invited participants who were not my students. Second, I hosted the meetings in my home and provided a meal. Third, I had no formal role in evaluating these students. Finally, I tried not to intervene in participants' decisions about where to position themselves as they gathered in my living room for dinner, what themes and topics to pursue in the conversations, or whose remarks to favor or follow up on in discussion.

Despite these efforts, the fieldnotes I kept and my subsequent review of the audiotapes I collected showed me that I did not ever really evade a leadership role. I had chosen the books and planned the sequence in which they were read. And, although I was a host, I was also a professor. Adding to the distance between the other members and myself, they knew that I wanted to study our conversations. And, lest they forget, a tape recorder was unobtrusively situated just below the coffee table. Reviews and analysis of the taped conversations pointed up moments when I assisted or blundered in on potentially educative book talk about culture. Sometimes I was aware at the time I made these conversational moves. But often I was not. My tacit instructional participation underscored the difficulty of altering the "default mode" of classroom discourse, even in explicitly alternative and supportive settings and activities.

However, I did not come away from the Future Teachers' Autobiography Club with a sense that teaching was unnecessary to learning about culture in autobiography and conversation. In fact, I identified in analyses of the transcripts many moments of opportunity where a teacher might, indeed, have intervened to support and extend learning in the conversations. Just like the youngsters whom my interns and I hoped would learn mathematical reasoning, this project underscored for me the difficulty of learning about culture, and the need, even in literacy events that are peer-led and response-oriented, for teachers and teaching. However, as chapter 7 addresses, my watching and listening as a teacher and, subsequently, the nature, content, and timing of my instructional moves might be far different given a closer look at book talk in the Autobiography Club.

Knowing a bit more about how and what we talked about when we talked about culture—and what were our limitations and particular frustrations—led to some alternate ways of thinking about teaching in this context. In this way, the work among adults in book clubs parallels the prior work on youngsters' book clubs, where instruction does not evaporate but changes, often dramatically, in its content, forms, and functions (Raphael & Hiebert, 1996). Some of these moments of insight about teaching are described in the next three chapters. They are important to me because they suggest ways in which teachers and teacher educators can and do have a role in fostering educative talk about culture.

## About the Other Club Members

As was mentioned the outset of this book, all members were Euro-American women from the midwest and in their early 20s. Table 4.1 summarizes their home communities in terms of socioeconomic status (SES) and lists their research pseudonyms. Two were from lower income small towns, two from the upper income suburbs of large cities, and two from middle

**TABLE 4.1.** *Student Members of the Future Teachers' Autobiography Club and Their Home Communities*

| Name/Pseudonym | Home Community |
| --- | --- |
| Nell and Misty | Affluent suburbs of large cities |
| Peggy and Lia | Lower income small towns |
| Marcia and Julie | Middle income suburbs of small cities |

income suburbs of smaller cities. They resembled in age, gender, race, and socioeconomic background the teachers who dominate elementary education in the United States. It is impossible to say from this limited work either how more diverse book club conversations might look or how participants different from this club's membership in race, gender, first language, or SES might have experienced the conversations.[1] My recruitment of White female teacher candidates has been critiqued on this basis (Pailliotet, 1995), and can also be criticized for perpetuating a genre of research on teacher thinking that reifies the characteristics of the mainstream teaching force by the informants it selects.

Notwithstanding these limitations, my decision was based on several considerations, both pragmatic and theoretical. First, the teacher education cohort from whom I recruited participants was exclusively White and female. Second, the predominantly Euro-American females in elementary education will serve as gatekeepers for the next generation of teachers. Third, emerging research on "Whiteness" and on the discourse practices of White middle class women suggested that exploration of difference might be an especially challenging task for this population. Yet, as McLaren (1997) observes, it is precisely its invisibility that must be addressed if teachers are to learn about racism and construct a practice that is anti-racist.

In order for cultural study to be more than curricular window dressing, McLaren argues that teachers need to explore the racist bases of colonialism, economic inequality, and the diversity of experience in the U.S. democratic system depending on one's race, gender, ethnicity, first lan-

---

[1]In a recent related doctoral dissertation, Reischl (1999) studied a book club more culturally and linguistically diverse. The group she studied met at a multilingual elementary school and included both intern and experienced teachers among its members.

guage, or social background. Was this apparently homogeneous group of young women entirely without resources to explore race and culture within a book club? Given that teaching is not merely telling, might there be a way that they could learn about racism and cultural inequality in authentically engaging activity? Could differences we might identify as we read and talked about a diverse literature of life stories help us to see what had hitherto been invisible in our own socialization? As both practitioner and researcher, I was curious to find out.

For all their apparent similarities, the members of the Future Teachers' Autobiography Club differed in terms of the relative size, wealth, and expectations of the communities in which they lived and were schooled. Nell and Misty came from affluent suburbs of large cities. Misty's father was a teacher, and she attended a well-known, elite public high school near Chicago. Nell attended private schools in the suburbs of Detroit. Both were groomed for college life. Misty was the only student in the group who had not grown up in Michigan. She was making a transition away from home and from an urban setting to an agricultural one. Nell, on the other hand, was juggling multiple life changes. She was recently married, newly pregnant, and still grieving the death of her mother several years earlier in an automobile accident.

Peggy and Lia were about to become the first persons in their families to complete college. Each came from lower income small towns—Lia from an agricultural town on the outskirts of the university community and Peggy from the rural Upper Peninsula of the state. Neither experienced strong support from their families to pursue education after high school. Both lamented the academic preparation their economically strapped rural schools had provided. Peggy had recently spent the summer working at a camp near Detroit where she was the only counselor who was not African American. She was now romantically involved with a fellow counselor and thinking about race in new, more intense ways. Lia, on the other hand, recently married a man from her home community. Somewhat older than the others, she had returned to college to become a teacher. Her noncollege-educated husband's uneasiness with her choice seemed to cloud her young marriage.

Marcia and Julie came from middle income suburbs of small cities. Both were enjoying the intellectual challenge of university work and were beginning more fully to experience themselves as teachers and intellectuals. However, both brought with them to the university experiences of loss and transformation. Marcia still felt strongly about her family's move to Michigan from the southwest when she was in elementary school.

Although she believed her family would like her to remain in Michigan after graduation, she longed to attend graduate school in Colorado. Julie was also originally from the southwest. Currently, she was planning a wedding, and her future husband was applying to medical schools. She juggled her identity as a college student, future teacher, and fiancée with her role as a daughter in a nearby extended family including her mother, stepfather, two sisters, and a half-sister. As I got to know the members of this group, I was as struck by its diversity as I was by its apparent homogeneity.

## TRANSFORMING OUR TEXTS AND CONTEXTS

Finding and examining a rich array of texts from which teachers can learn about culture is a challenge for our profession. Teacher educators have been experimenting for the past two decades with oral and personal narrative as sources for teacher learning (e.g., Butt & Raymond, 1987; Clandinnin & Connelly, 1987; Grumet, 1980; Schubert, 1991). Others are exploring a range of literary genres (including poetry and drama) to represent teachers' remembered life experience in compelling ways (Salvio, 1990). Autobiography occurred to me as a useful genre quite by accident. I joined a book club in my neighborhood public library in 1992. The head librarian, a woman expert in ethnic literature, led it, and we read and discussed many books that might best be called "autobiographical novels" (Morrison, 1992, p. vi).

Epitomized by Mukherjee's (1989) novel, *Jasmine*, these books recounted immigration stressing continuous interplay of setting, relationships, and dramatic action in the immigrant's ongoing reinvention of herself. These books shed light on home—the one that was left, the one that is entered, and the home we each carry with us as we make new encounters. The books we read in the library book club were not dry accounts of the facts of a life or a culture but dramatic recreations of life and culture that moved the reader. They called forth response from their narrative design that is described by Toni Morrison (1992), another author who has experimented with this form, as their "flashbacks, well-placed descriptive passages, carefully placed action, and timely discoveries" (p. vi).

This literature provided some of the point of view and moral tension I had found wanting in the social science reports I had written and read in my work as a teacher and researcher. Additionally, talking about books in the informal atmosphere of an adult book club (with its interplay of casual conversation, genial banter and contesting over interpretations, and personal vignettes echoing the book's themes) was stimulating. It contrasted sharply with what typically passes for book talk among not only schoolchildren in reading groups, but secondary and college students' classroom-based literary discussion (Marshall, Smagorinsky, & Smith, 1995).

## Autobiography: Changing the Text

There is a growing autobiographical literature dealing with diverse authors' coming of age as teachers and learners. In this literature, the reader is invited to share the experiences of literacy and learning voiced by men and women who vary in race, ethnicity, cultural and economic background, and first language. This is, not surprisingly, a literature of strong and mixed emotions. It chronicles the freeing and enabling experience of learning new knowledge in a new language code, as well as the silence and humiliation of participating in groups and activities where what one already knows, values, and can express is ignored or rejected by others.

I identified the autobiographies read by the Future Teachers' Autobiography Club using a simple set of criteria: First, I wanted the future teachers to read books that viewed cultural experience through the lens of personal narrative. The authors whose books I chose crafted life stories as literary texts. These books enabled close and contrastive examination of the experiences of diverse Americans and invited exploration of autobiography as a genre for recording and representing experience. They fostered talk about what defines us, makes us different from one another, and binds us as human beings. Second, I chose full-length autobiographical books rather than autobiographical essays or excerpts. I wanted participants to read extended accounts of experience by of immigrants living in the United States across considerable differences in background. Third, I wanted participants to sample autobiographies along a continuum from experiences close in proximity those distant from their own.

The autobiographies I selected were of three types. One pair was written by Euro-American teachers who, encountering diverse pupils, were challenged to examine their own lives and learning through the lens of culture—Vivian Paley's (1979/1989) *White Teacher* and Mike Rose's (1989) *Lives on the Boundary*. Two books were written by immigrants who came voluntarily to the United States seeking and finding (although

not without cost) security, education and economic opportunity—Eva
Hoffman's (1989) *Lost in Translation* and Jill Ker Conway's (1989) *The
Road from Coorain*. Completing the set were two autobiographies by
American-born authors fitting anthropologist John Ogbu's (1987) classifi-
cation, "involuntary immigrants," or people who came (or whose forebears came) to the United States as slaves or economic refugees and have
been subject to race-based "caste-like" minority status with attendant discrimination in education and employment. These books were Richard
Rodriguez's (1982) *Hunger of Memory* and Maya Angelou's (1969) *I
Know Why the Caged Bird Sings*. I hoped that the comparisons and contrasts implicit and explicit in this "text set" (Calkins, 1991, pp. 132–133)
would stand-in for ethnographic contacts with the diverse cultural experiences of others. In choosing autobiography to learn about culture, we were
encountering an alternative literary genre. Talking about them in book
clubs, we were participating in an alternative "speech genre" (Bakhtin,
1986).

## Conversation: Transforming the Context

Central to the book club experience was conversation as a site for readers'
comprehension and response. *Conversation* is a useful image to characterize both teacher learning and the literacy education of pupils. By conversation, I refer to the dialogic process by which we create and negotiate
meaning. Defined this way, conversation is a primary means by which
educators do their work. We hold different kinds of conversations for different purposes, and the nature and structure of our conversation varies
across situation and cultural context. However, for the purposes of education, I think of conversation in its simplest terms as, in Van Manen's
(1977) words, "a type of dialogue which is not adversarial but, as
Socrates expressed it, 'like friends talking together'" (p. 218). To that definition I would add, "about their ideas." In an open memo to his students,
educational philosopher Nash (n.d.) describes educational conversation's
friendly yet deliberative nature as follows:

> The word, *conversation*, comes from the Latin, *conversari*, which means: to live
> with, keeps company with, to turn around, to oppose. Thus, conversation is liter-
> ally a manner of living whereby people keep company with each other, and talk
> together, in good faith, formally and informally, in order to exchange opposing
> ideas. . . . The interchange continues at its best when the participants are not
> impatient to conclude their business, but wish instead to spend their time

together in order to deepen and enrich their understanding of an idea, or, in our case, the ideas in a text. (p. 3)

Educators are interested in conversation's role in learning, especially the learning of literacy (Gavelek & Raphael, 1996). Psychologists researching the learning process, for example, cite the writings of Vygotsky (1978), who posited that higher order reasoning, or "inner speech," begins as conversation with more experienced others, or "social speech." Bakhtin (1986), whose literary theories stressed the mingling and multiplicity of voices and variation in meaning dependent on social context, is read by students not only of fiction, but also of the social organization of communication schools and other cultural settings. These theories reverberate in the contemporary American classroom and its curriculum. Teachers are encouraged to support writing development in conferences, workshops, and other forms of talk about student text. Reading comprehension is construed for purposes of instruction as a process of meaning construction dependent on conversation-like transaction among reader, text, and author. Current methods of teaching mathematics and science stress the development of higher order reasoning in students' problem-solving discussion. Even in educational research, where traditionally teachers and pupils were "subjects," practitioners are now encouraged to converse across boundaries once separating them from researchers to frame questions, gather data, and craft analyses of their own practice.

Paralleling this movement in educational theory and practice are strong calls from the field of teacher education to transform its own dominant paradigm from knowledge transmission to knowledge construction (Lieberman & Miller, 1991). Noting a "deficit model" in teacher education where practitioners are assumed to be "unthinking," Griffin (1991) urges that teacher education shift from teaching by telling (i.e., where experts disseminate information about instruction to disempowered workers) to learning by talking (i.e., where teacher learning occurs in thoughtful dialogue among empowered professional peers). With this shift, planning and reflection join instruction as essential components of a teacher's self-directed professional activity. According to Griffin (1991):

research on teacher thinking, on teachers' implicit theories, and on expert teachers supports a view of teachers as persons who are thoughtful about their work, their impact on students, their strong points and their vulnerabilities. This research, in part, also points out how teachers, particularly veterans, are often less than precise about these thoughts and considerations, in large part because of the absence of any need to become articulate, to be communicative, to use the thoughts as objects of systematic attention with their colleagues. (p. 248)

Treating teachers as unknowing or inarticulate about their practice and its problems creates a damaging self-fulfilling prophecy. Griffin argues for changing this troubling dynamic by means of conversation or "interactive staff development" in which, in his words, "the stories teachers tell, the successes they recount, the frustrations and dilemmas they face would become a significant source of ideas for improvement or change or 'reform' activity" (p. 248).

## ENGAGING LITERACY IN COMMUNITY

Much like their pupils, teachers traditionally learn in instructional settings where story and dialogue are absent. This is the case for their early schooling and much of their higher education. McDiarmid (1989), for example, finds little in the undergraduate curriculum encouraging educative discussion. Because, in his words,

lecturing appears to dominate instruction at the university level as it does at the secondary level, students rarely are forced to state, much less to examine, defend or justify their beliefs or ideas. Consequently, while they may remember what a lecturer has said in order to pass a test, the information they commit to short-term memory may not alter their own frameworks for making sense of the world, of themselves, and of others. Their deeply rooted beliefs and conceptions . . . remain untouched by the words of text or teacher. (p. 6)

This experience limits teachers' sense of dialogue's possibilities. It further reinforces their assumptions about what it means to teach, how it students learn, and the role of talk and text in these processes. Urged in their courses to make learning engaging and meaningful for youngsters, teacher candidates do not always experience the same purpose and engagement in their own learning. Reflecting on her recollections of learning to read, one teacher candidate told me the following:

I felt like I hated reading. I was reading the same thing repeatedly. I was thinking of how this book [a basal] was like the merry-go-round; it always did the same things. I was reading so the teacher could hear me utter the words correctly, not to get a meaning from the words. I was supposedly reading. I was not thinking about deriving meaning from the text as a first grader, and I know I was not enjoying reading. Reading these books was something I had to do to satisfy my teacher and I did it.[2]

Such a view of reading and school learning precludes discussion of ideas as part of comprehension. The text is of minimal interest, so thin that it provides little fodder for discussion. Conversation is restricted to the teacher posing factual recall questions, nominating individual students to answer them, and recycling the question in search of a better answer or moving on to the next question and speaker. This "merry-go-round" is reinforced throughout the student's education so that eventually she equates books (and book talk) with irrelevancy and monotony. Speaking of her alienation from books, another teacher candidate speculated as follows on what she hoped to do differently when she took charge of her own class:

I expect to give my students the ability and desire to learn. I don't want them to dread coming to school every day. I want them to be excited and anxious to learn new things. I would hope to accomplish this by having them do many creative, hands-on activities with each other and eliminating a lot of textbook and busy work. With textbooks, students may get some information. But from my past experience, I think what they learn there is easily forgotten and often not very well understood. Just as you can't learn to ride a bike by reading a book, you can't learn geography and science [from books] very well either.

It is hard to argue with this future teacher's conviction that learning should be meaningful and engaging to youngsters, but her comments offer troubling images of literacy and the relationship of books to ideas and authentic or "hands-on" learning. Rejecting the way she was taught leads her to devalue literacy as she envisions the classrooms for which she will be responsible. However, once she begins to assume responsibility for teaching she will find that decisions about text are unavoidable.

Beginners who teach with and about books only grudgingly have few alternatives when confronted with responsibility for literacy instruction. Many default to the exclusive use of the school's preordained basal series or, when trade books are available, treating them as if they were basals. The depersonalized book talk to which they once reacted with disdain is

---

[2]Learning Community Teacher Education Program Pre-service Teacher Survey (1990).

so deeply woven into the fabric of classroom and school culture that, without explicit intervention, beginners intuitively reproduce it despite their better intentions. Describing this powerful model, Eeds and Wells (1989) note the following:

> all popular basal stories provide students with readers constraining stories (many excerpted from fine literature) and teachers with questions (and accompanying answers) to ask about those stories. Children gather together in groups to discuss the stories, but discussion usually consists of the teacher asking the questions and the children attempting to answer them. Their comprehension of the story is judged by how closely their answers match those in the textbook. (p. 4)

This model of reading and discussion places minimal importance on the appreciation or interpretation of literary text. The texts read by students are typically controlled for grade-level difficulty either by the modification of original works of literature or by the invention of nonliterary text explicitly for comprehension instruction.

Rosen (1987) argues that this kind of simplification does not enhance instruction but rather distorts it, abridging the integrity of text and precluding young readers applying their own narrative understanding, what he deems "a cognitive resource—a meaning-making strategy" (p. 13). Additionally, with little sustenance in talk or the text, students are rarely challenged to sustain intellectually demanding literate activities. Thus, they fail to experience a sense of accomplishment in their own learning or the support for learning that comes from dialogue with others. Teachers' reliance on text-based recitation curtails students' speaking rights, limiting their opportunities to construct meaning narratively and in dialogue with others. Citing numerous recent studies of classroom discourse, Rosen notes that

> the further up the school system we go the less likely is it that spontaneous, pupil-made narrative will be able to insert itself comfortably and naturally into the flow of talk. For in most classrooms the chief and privileged storyteller (stories of any kind) is the teacher. The right to tell stories of any kind is invisibly conferred on her and the exploitation of that right is very limited. (pp. 17–18)

Although it is commonplace to encourage teachers to create "communities of learning" in their classroom (e.g., our teacher education program took its name from Schwab's, 1976, essay on "Learning Community"), we often ask this of teachers without sufficient attention to their preparation and lacking sufficient understanding of the educational point of doing so. Burbules (1993) observes in this regard that

> exhorting teachers to engage in various liberatory practices, as many progressive educational theorists do, without also providing a realistic means to acquire, reflect upon, and improve those practices has often had the effect of discouraging teachers more than inspiring them. (p. x)

Yet, although there are many studies of classroom recitation (see Cazden, 1988, for a summary), to date relatively few researchers have examined in depth the dynamics of communication in conversational learning arrangements, either teacher-led or among peers. These approaches are popular, but as O'Connor and Michaels (1993) observe, "we do no currently have adequate theoretical apparatus to characterize the complexity—at both a cognitive and social level—of these more open-ended sense making discussions" (p. 7).

By studying the Autobiography Club, I hoped to enter the uncharted waters of this theorizing by asking three questions:

- What are participants saying about culture, literacy, and schooling as they discuss the autobiographies?
- How do they interpret the books in relation to their own lives as teachers and learners?
- What are the club's conversational dynamics?

Chapter 5 describes the process by which I researched these questions in collaboration with Julie deTar.

# CHAPTER 5

# Inquiry
# Into Autobiography
# and Conversation

From the first meeting of the Future Teachers' Autobiography Club onward, I collected and reviewed meeting tapes, fieldnotes, and the writing done in members' sketchbooks. As I did this, I framed, pursued, and revised, what Geer (1969) called "working hypotheses." These hunches framed and focused my investigation of the ways participants were talking and apparently making sense of the books and conversations. I also used a research method called "constant comparison" (Glaser & Strauss, 1967), which involves rejecting or refining early interpretations based on the examination of subsequent data. By means of "triangulation" (Gordon, 1980), I tested inferences that I developed in one data source (e.g., field-notes) with information available in other data sources (e.g., meeting transcripts, sketchbooks, and debriefing interviews). And, as is characteristic of ethnographic work, I often got things wrong from the point of view of participants' experience despite all of these efforts. Thus, as is also characteristic of ethnographic work, focus of the research changed and developed as the study progressed, and the analysis ultimately benefited from a research collaboration with Julie deTar.

## EARLY INTERPRETATION:
## CONNECTED KNOWERS?

I was initially impressed by the cooperative nature of the club's conversation and missed the conflicts underlying its sociable talk. At first glance, the participants seemed to offer personal narratives in response to the published ones and coordinate them with one another across turns. I conjectured that this cooperative, narrative way of speaking about the books would prove to be a distinctive feature of club discourse. A similar speech style was reported in research on White women's talk in therapeutic and consciousness-raising (or "rap") groups and strengthened my conjecture (Aries, 1976). Kalcik's (1975) research, for example, found that participants avoided interrupting or challenging one another's ideas. They typically offered brief personal vignettes as "kernel stories," not to "one up" other speakers, but to elaborate on their comments.

I reviewed research on women's speech in small, informal, same-gender settings, including literary, therapeutic, and consciousness-raising groups (Coates & Cameron, 1989; Edelsky, 1993; Gere, 1997; Gernes, 1992; Jenkins & Kramer, 1978; Jordan & Kalcik, 1985; Tannen, 1993), thinking that our dinner conversations might bear a family resemblance to these. Research in these settings finds more acceptance of personal narrative than is generally the case in school talk about text. I noticed that the book club conversations tended to unfold as narrative "rounds" in which members exchanged turns by acknowledging the remarks of the previous speaker and taking them as a point of departure for her own. These comments often took the form of thematically linked vignettes, giving the conversations a sense of connection and mutual support. Often this talk stressed personal or moral implications of a work of literature rather than analysis of it based on literary critical "close reading" of the text as free-standing and interpreted solely in terms of its figurative language (see, e.g., Brooks, 1947).

A mainstay of literature study in high school and college classrooms, versions of close reading appear widely and are the inheritance of most of us who have become teachers. And, although attention to the craft of writing is also valued, contemporary critics point out that the rigors of close reading leave the reader's experience and the author's intention out. In the bargain, the negotiated nature of meaning—that of author, reader, and the interpretive communities whose literary resources each employs, is not available for study (Freund, 1987).

In contrast to this style of reading, the book club participants preferred talking about a text's themes and their relationship to the readers' own lives. Thus, they echoed the form and function of women's talks in other book club of the past described by Gere (1997). Moreover, in their com-plementary quality of linking and building on the spoken and written texts of authors and conversational partners, they embodied in both style and substance what Belenky, Clinchy, Goldberger, and Tarule (1986) identify as U.S., middle-class women's penchant for "connected knowing." How-ever, as the following examples illustrate, participants' inclusion of their own narratives in response to the published autobiographies did not pre-clude their examination of the writer's craft, a text's structural properties, or the thematic content of the published narratives. Instead, these conver-sations unfolded as hybrid literacy events in which voices and styles of reading and responding mingled.

## THE SITUATION AND CONTEXT

Neither a seminar nor a support group, nor a dinner party, the Autobiogra-phy Club, as a hybrid speech situation lacked clear and explicit rules for participation. It required members to negotiate a definition of situation in and through conversation in an ongoing way. Although the club's immedi-ate social context bore resemblance to several familiar speech events, book club conversations looked, sounded, and felt different both from researchers' descriptions of school-based discussion of literature (e.g., Applebee, 1990; Marshall, 1989; Marshall et al., 1995), and also the stud-ies of women's informal conversations just described.

Classroom book talk assumes a group that already has a clear teacher-leader. That person controls access to turns and keeps talk focused on the topic in question. In research on high school discussion of literature, for example, there is a predominance of talk directly about the text's features (e.g., style, tone, plot, theme, etc.) while autobiographical commentary (either about author or reader) is discouraged and relatively rare (Mar-shall, 1989). Talk advances in large part by a teacher's questions about the book, with students bidding for an opportunity to reply and the teacher responding to evaluate student replies thus moving the dialogue along to a recycling of the initial question or to a new round of question framing and answering. Rarely in this format would a student initiate a question about a book or initiate a round of student responses—narrative or otherwise. Moreover, although infrequently exercised, the classroom rights to talk about personal experience in relation to a text accrue almost exclusively to the teacher (Marshall, 1989).

In contrast, research on women's speech in informal settings predicts that participants will admit to more personal narrative in their talk. They would be likely to exchange turns by acknowledging the remarks of a previous speaker and building on them, thus sharing conversational leadership by combining viewpoints rather than arguing for a single interpretation. Thus, informal talk about books would maximize sharing (or at least the negotiation) of leadership, personal response, and the production of coordinating rather than competing ideas across turns. Interestingly, however, full-blown narratives would be as unexpected in book clubs as they would be inside classrooms. In informal, small group conversation, extended narratives are avoided due to sanctions against participants dominating talk and topical agenda. Participants frequently offer incomplete or "kernel" narratives rather than full-blown ones. These serve to personalize responses and move conversations along by offering subsequent speakers incomplete texts onto which to map their, presumably coordinating, turns.

The book club blended the affiliative work one would expect to see in conversation among friends with the deliberative work of framing and answering questions one might expect in school. We seemed to find our way largely by use of extended personal narratives that thematically surround the book under discussion. On many occasions, participants talked about the published lives in terms of extensive accounts of their own life experiences, thus blending book talk and self-talk. Sociolinguists studying conversational involvement find that participants show engagement and create continuity by carefully monitoring previous speakers' turns and appropriating from them themes, text structure, images and even particular words (Tannen, 1989). In book club talk, these strategies apply not only to previous speakers' turns, but also to the texts in question.

This style of book talk seems dangerously close to the kind of talk I used to discourage in my middle school language arts class. More about the reader than the text, this kind of talk was usually taken as a sure sign that my students had not finished reading the assignment, or at least had not read it carefully. But in our book club, the sketchbooks were scribbled upon with noteworthy quotes and page numbers, the book's pages were turned down in select places, and participants read most of the books avidly, cover to cover. Still, members persisted in talking about the books narratively and in terms of their own lives.

Although such "talk about self" as a form of literary response is growing in use and esteem among teachers (Probst, 1988), it left me with a vague sense that we were not thinking critically about the text. Moreover, with so much continuity among speakers' topics and turn exchange, and so much apparent connecting of their narrative responses to the book, I wondered if we might not be able to break free of our connected knowledge to look at our differences. This move seemed essential if we were to break the frame of our assumptions about our own homogeneity, the culturally unmarked nature of our beliefs and ways of speaking, and the racially and socially isolated nature of the teaching role.

## A RESEARCH COLLABORATION

In the summer of 1994, after the Future Teachers' Autobiography Club had disbanded and its members graduated, Julie deTar, a former club member, volunteered to collaborate on the data analysis. I had shared preliminary analyses of our club's conversations with the members, and although most received them with nodding interest, the picture of book club conversation and learning they painted troubled at least one member. Although I was a participant in the book club, I was not a classmate of the six student teachers. I lacked prior knowledge of the relationships these young women had formed during their preservice education. Moreover, I did not have access to them between meetings. Although in some ways an insider, I remained outside many of their experiences.

Julie was much closer to the other five club members, having studied with them over 2 years in the Learning Community program. As such, she knew they each brought histories and social identities negotiated over months of interactions with one another. The politics of their talk, however politely expressed, was conflictual. And their conflicts spilled over into the book talk at my home. Julie believed that we might be able to learn more from the book club if we could look more closely at struggle as it was evidenced in the conversational dynamics of the group—in their silences, in their responses to the books, and in their responses to one another.

It was Julie's insight that participants' apparently smooth shifting from speaker to speaker and their mapping of personal narratives on one another should not be confused with consensus or even a supportive climate. Sometimes, she observed, participants showed resistance to an idea by not speaking. Sometimes they spoke supportively in the hope that a speaker would be sufficiently satisfied to relinquish the floor. Often, she said, "you had to work hard just to stay involved" in the complex discussions. Julie felt that my preliminary analyses focused too much on connection and continuity and therefore did not capture her experience of what she termed participants' *struggle* to engage each other, the books, and the issues they raised about race, ethnicity, language, and social class.

*Struggle* is a term that appears often in academic discussions of dialogue (see Burbules, 1993, for a summary; and Chavez Chavez & O'Donnell, 1998). It can refer quite literally to different speakers in conflict within a conversation or to multiple, often contested, meanings a term or text may reflect. It further captures a dynamic of the genre of autobiography's concern with multiple representations of self (Lionnet, 1989; Zuss, 1997). Thus, Julie alerted me to the problem of reasoning from surface features of politeness and engagement that consensus exists. We can engage on the common ground of conversation without being of a common mind. Involvement strategies used by speakers (Tannen, 1989) are part of what Burbules (1993) calls the "conversational virtues" (p. x) that keep talk smoothly and civilly flowing. As such, they can be thought of as a means rather than an end. Without attention to politeness and engagement, conversation would grind to a halt. Yet what was it we were conversing about? And how might we identify the struggles that might lead to learning?

With the permission of the book club's other former members, Julie and I worked together during the ensuing school year to analyze audiotapes and transcripts of the club's conversations. One of the conversations during which Julie identified a great deal of struggle around the idea of culture occurred when we discussed Richard Rodriguez's autobiography, *Hunger of Memory*. On this night, readers' prior experiences were important in their responses to the book. It was in narrating these experiences that book club members revealed some of what makes their own lives different from the lives of those seated with them at the table. In so doing, however, they also traversed a complicated landscape of experiences like and unlike their own, complicating and enriching their conceptual mappings of the idea of "culture." Chief among the themes their narratives raised were the following:

1.  Learning new ways of communicating as a function of formal education.
2.  Loss as one makes a life transition.
3.  Cultural contact and change.
4.  Social class as a determiner of access to education.

5. Acquiescence or resistance to cultural norms in the groups of which one is a member.

These themes are further described in the next chapter, and narratives told by book club members to illustrate them are included in the appendix.

Participants told a set of coordinating narratives echoing a key theme in Rodriguez's book: moving between worlds and the loss and lack of authenticity one may feel in this process. Either directly or vicariously, they encircled this theme with stories. Even those finding Rodriguez's image of the "scholarship boy" less than credible gradually began to explore the idea in story. Rodriguez's book presses this point, permitting no easy escape from the consequences of cross-cultural contact. These student teachers have not experienced directly economic or social discrimination on the basis of race or first language, but they reached into their experience for instances when they or someone close to them felt the pain of alienation, the difficulty of moving between two worlds, and the loss of a sense of home. Thus, it can also argued, as Paley (1979/1989) does in her book *White Teacher*, that in discovering ways to access and represent the sense of another's experience, we may begin to move from professing cultural understanding to knowing ourselves and others more fully.

To identify and analyze the narratives told in the book club conversation, Julie and I adapted Marshall et al.'s (1995) construct of the "episode" (or series of thematically connected speaker turns) as an analytic tool. Calling our unit of analysis the "narrative episode," we coded the meeting transcripts for sequences within which a speaker (or several speakers in coordinating turns) rendered a full or partial story within the context of the ongoing club conversation. We defined a narrative episode either as an extended turn in which one speaker offered a narrative or as a topically connected set of turns in which multiple speakers told a narrative. Narratives were either freestanding or full-blown stories moving from problem framing to conclusion, or were partial stories, "kernels" from which other speakers developed related ones (Kalcik, 1975). Tracking discussion of culture in these narratives, we noted participants offering individual or jointly constructed accounts of culture as a process of identification transformed over time and in light of social, political, and economic circumstances. The narratives approached culture as socially negotiated, situated, and relative. We used the narrative episode construct to code our tapes and transcripts.

Adapting Erickson and Shultz's micro ethnographic research method of the researcher/informant "viewing session" (Denyer & Florio-Ruane,

1995; Erickson & Shultz, 1975; Florio & Walsh, 1981), we held listening sessions in which we read the transcripts together as we listened to the audiotapes of book club conversations. The purpose of this activity was to foster dialogue among a student participant (Julie) and a participant-observer somewhat more distanced from the group's dynamics (myself). In this way, we were working back and forth from an insider and outsider stance—what linguist Pike (1967) calls "emic" and "etic" perspectives— to try to discover more of the local meaning and complexity in the book clubs than I alone would have been able to interpret. We did this not to create interrater reliability but, as a study ethnographic in its design, to foster the "self–other dialogue" that anthropologists believe is crucial to fieldwork (B. Tedlock, 1991).

Our analysis of the club's 6 monthly book club conversations revealed high density of narrative episodes. Story-related talk accounts for anywhere from slightly more than one fourth to over one half of all turns taken during the meetings. We coded the narrative episodes as personal, teacher, book, and other. These categories refer to the topic of the episode. In some cases, participants told narratives about their current or past experiences in their relationships with friends or family members. We coded these as personal narratives. In other cases, participants told stories in which they recounted experiences in their capacities as student teachers. These were coded as teacher narratives. When participants retold vignettes from the published books, we coded them as book-related narratives. A small group of narratives in each meeting seemed not to fit any one of these three major categories (e.g., a vignette about the difficulty of getting to the meeting due to weather; a vignette about the host's dog), and these we categorized as other.

On any given night, a high proportion of our talk took the form of narratives told in response to the book. However, as the semester of student teaching unfolds, participants' talk about their teaching grows more prominent and intense. We see an increase in the number of narratives told in which the topic is their experience of some aspect of student teaching and the position they take as they narrate is that of "teacher." Thus, participants appeared to be mining their past and current experiences for vignettes to tell in response to the themes and issues raised by the books. In doing this, they traversed the terrain of "identity"—moving between what Nias (1989) calls their "situational selves" of the here and now and their "substantive" selves or an "inner core" of assumptions about themselves that are difficult to access, talk about, and change (paraphrased from Nias, 1989, pp. 20–21). In addition to exploring situational and inner selves, they narrated "possible selves," those identities they might avow in the future as they grew in knowledge and experience as teachers (P. Conway, 1998).

Table 5.1 illustrates that, on the night we met to discuss *Hunger of Memory*, more than one fourth of all speaking turns involved the telling of narratives. Of these, there was a preponderance of teacher narratives. Coming at the time in the semester when participants were holding their first parent conferences, many of these concern the narrator's experiences with diverse families, particularly those of youngsters struggling to learn literacy. Participants told stories from their perspective as teacher 44% of the time. They also told stories of themselves as pupils or learners 25% of the time. Taken together, this profile suggests a strong concern on that occasion with their own and others' experience of the transition from home to school. Additionally, the participants retold vignettes from the book related to this theme. Nearly 25% of the narrative episodes directly concerned the book, making Rodriguez's words, images, and viewpoint strongly present in the conversation.

Wortham (1995) studied the way a person's identity is represented in the narratives told by self and other in conversations. He contends that narrators can play a role in shaping the self by the stories in which they present themselves or talk about others. The very act of telling a story of self in dialogue with others combines a story's theme with its performance as an act of speaking. By the discursive mix of story, self, other, and conversation, we show ourselves to ourselves and also to others. Thought of this way, the book club is an emergent and jointly constructed text, an autobiography-in-process, a potentially powerful cocktail for teachers' learning about themselves and the teaching role.

With narrative carrying the bulk of the conversational freight, our book club talk might be mistaken for informal conversation among friends. But on closer examination, we found that in those stories participants wove personal response, examination of identity, analysis of the author's craft and the structure of his or her text, and exploration of the text's moral themes. This is the kind of talk about text researchers who have studied women's book talk outside the walls of the university contend is not only characteristic, but is important intellectual work (Gernes, 1992). Women's book clubs, in Gere's (1997) analysis, contributed a genre of to literature study to our scholarship that might otherwise have been missed within academic literary criticism and school-based book talk. And, for our purposes,

**TABLE 5.1** *Narrative Analysis of Discussion of* Hunger of Memory

| | |
|---|---|
| Total narrative episodes | 48 |
| Teacher | 21 (44%) |
| Personal | 12 (25%) |
| Book | 11 (23%) |
| Other | 4 (8%) |
| Total turns | 335 |
| Total narrative—related turns | 95 |
| % Narrative—related talk | 28% |

book clubs frame and focus themes and issues of moral valence that are of great importance to us as teachers, learners, and citizens.

Thus, while new to those of us who participated in these autobiography clubs, book clubs are far from new in the lives of American women of diverse backgrounds. When Gere (1997) conducted a detailed history of women's book clubs at the turn of the century, she looked at reading, writing, and talk about text in range of social contexts and around a variety of cultural projects. If we substitute the term *teachers* for *women* in her comment that follows, we begin to get a sense of how book clubs like the Future Teachers' Autobiography Club might function as a community of learning professionals in which autobiography and conversation play powerful roles in cultural transformation:

> Women's clubs were part of public life, but as intermediate institutions located between the family and the state, they also fostered intimacy among members. That is, clubs had political as well as personal dimensions, and literacy figured prominently in both. Although clubs occupied a subordinate political position, they offered strong and creative resistance to that subordination through literacy practices that cultivated the making of meaning in the company of others. (p. 13)

Reading and responding to text in the Future Teachers' Autobiography Club stands in contrast to conventional academic practice in teacher education and staff development as well as in literature study. Because of its potential for learning both about literacy and culture in complex, critical, and dialogic ways, the book club constitutes a learning environment worthy of continued study. Therefore, as teachers as well as researchers, Julie and I were drawn to its narratives for a closer look. What kind of learning might they reveal? How did they function in and as conversation? What did they reveal about participants' presentations of themselves and their ideas about culture? The next chapter takes a closer look at the narrative episodes in light of these questions.

# CHAPTER 6

# Narrating Culture
# in Book Talk

The evening's book club began in consternation. We gathered to discuss Richard Rodriguez's book, *Hunger of Memory*. It took awhile for the conversation to find its way to the book. The club members were preoccupied by the pressures of their first parent conferences. Gradually, our discussion of communicating with parents encircled themes raised in Rodriguez's book, especially the complex relation between home and school when a child is learning at school in a new, second language. We lingered on the section describing "the scholarship boy" and the duality the image poses between home and school, private and public. Rodriguez (1982) says, for example,

> The scholarship boy must move between environments, his home and the classroom, which are at cultural extremes, opposed. With his family, the boy has the intense pleasure of intimacy, the family's consolation in feeling public alienation. Lavish emotions texture home life. *Then*, at school, the instruction bids him to trust lonely reason primarily. (p. 46)

As was discussed earlier in this book, as part of the "dominant culture," the members of our book club are comfortable with this trope as it explains other people's children. Most of us at the table experienced the transition from home to school as a relatively seamless one compared to the identity-wrenching transition Rodriguez describes. No change in language code was required of us, and we felt that family life groomed us, if not for university life, at least for going to elementary school.

Unaware of the extent to which our upbringing rehearsed primary school learning, Rodriguez's characterization of himself as a "scholarship boy"—eager to please, idolizing teachers, feeling ashamed of parents—initially seems artificial, even contrived. In raising the idea of the scholarship boy in his autobiography, Peggy comments that Rodriguez made a curious writing move. He shifts from writing in the first person to writing in the third person and from narrating his early school experience to critiquing it. In so doing, he generalizes from personal experience and embodies the tension between private and public that is thematically central to his book. Peggy bristles at this move. Taking issue with his pronominal shift, she rejects both Rodriguez' tactic and message saying,

> This is the first book I felt, I guess this is the first book I reacted so strongly against. I kept picking it back up around page sixty-five [where the idea of the scholarship boy is introduced] . . . and I would start there, and my mind was blocked and I tried to figure it out because . . . if you don't finish the book, why are you having trouble with it? But "the scholarship boy pleases" was. . . . I mean "scholarship boy"? I started thinking, this is *your* autobiography. Why are you writing about, is *that* something personal? You are not writing, "I." Why are you not writing, "I"? (Meeting Transcript, 3/25/93)

Peggy further argues that an autobiography is and should be about a person and, as such, should be single-voiced. To her, it is inappropriate for an autobiographer to step outside the personal to make social generalizations:

> I just got really angry, like I thought he was hiding. To be completely honest, if you are writing an autobiography, tell me about *you*. . . . I felt that there was holding back, that he was stepping out from himself when he said "the scholarship boy." That was my one hang up, you know, that he was stepping back to distance himself and not get really into it. (Meeting Transcript, 3/25/93)

Peggy's discomfort with Rodriguez's multivoiced writing style and his partitioning of private and public is shared by others at the meeting. His book is particularly troubling in the context of the upcoming parent conferences. The prospect of conflict or alienation between the home and school is unsettling to club members. Some advance a smooth, holistic image of "identity" as a reconciliation of multiple "selves." Rejecting the idea that people have a private self that can be different and perhaps alienated from their public self, Misty says, for example,

> You know how we . . . you wonder if he has like that private self still inside of him or whatever. You know that persons can have so many different selves to them. You know that you can have like this scholarly side, you can have the athletic side, you can have the quiet side of you, you can . . . it matters what turns out at the end. It just may be that this [the idea of the "scholarship boy"] is just the title that kind of defines a part of him. (Meeting Transcript, 3/25/93)

Yet if, as cultural psychologists Penuel and Wertsch (1996) argue, "self" is situated in activity and social history, then such a smooth coordination of "selves" is unlikely, particularly from people who are members of disenfranchised language-minority groups. Reaching for a connection to this possibility of alienation or conflict about identity in settings where as students they had little power, Julie and Marcia offer recollected experiences at school that echo Rodriguez's scholarship boy:

> **Julie:** I have felt that way . . . I always think of English class . . . all through high school I loved to read and stuff like that. I hate to analyze and I can do what he [Rodriguez] talks about where he will spit back exactly what the professor said to him. He would just spit back exactly what the professor said to him. He just spit back exactly what he read, didn't really do any of his own thinking. And that is how I went through high school English and got straight As. But in that English class where I tried to give my own ideas, finally, got squashed but I really felt like that.

> **Marcia:** It reminded me of myself and what school was like for me because I was always a straight A student, I mean first grade through college, and it was because I was that type of student . . . it was always doing what he did and getting so, you know, rewarded with great grades because of it. So, I know what you mean in that sense. I mean it is not so much of a stereotype. (Meeting Transcript, 3/25/96)

Interestingly, these example highlight schools' expectations of homogeneity of ideas, in the first case, and bias against high-achieving young women—by classmates, in the second. So, they bear some slight family resemblance to Rodriguez's trope, although they do so without talking about the issues of class, race, and language that underlie young Richard's feelings.

## EXTENSION
## INTO NEW MEANINGS

Some at the table are satisfied that by these extensions they have understood the author's point. Others are not. And, committed to one another and this conversation, we press onward. We are challenged by the conversation to think and speak a bit further. Faced with disagreement among themselves and with the author, the group pushes deeper to explore knowledge and beliefs about identity and culture. Davies and Harre (1990), in writing about the ways people's narratives socially locate, or position, the teller as well as the listener, refer to such interpretive efforts as "extensions." Extending or indexing new ideas to more familiar ones from our past is one way we make sense. This search for familiar ways of understanding is especially visible when people are confronted with narratives violating their extant assumptions about "who we are and what we are doing." Sometimes the discontinuity between what we already know and believe and the narrative confronting us is sufficient to prompt rethinking the familiar, telling ourselves a new story or retelling a familiar story from a new or different stance.

Rodriguez's narrative violates our book club's expectations. We are vulnerable to his criticisms of the liberal educational establishment and its solutions to educational inequality. Surprised by his political views, we realize or are inclined to stereotype others on the basis of features such as first language or ethnicity. Contrasting his narrative of going to school with our own experiences and recollections, we are aware of the relatively smooth transition from home to school we experienced as members of a socially and economically privileged group. Thus, we begin to recognize that our starting place as White, monolingual, and middle-class teachers is not an optimal position from which to understand the experiences of the diverse pupils and families with whom we now work. Responding to the book requires us to examine both Rodriguez's and our own personal narratives (and their embedded moral assumptions) about going to school, learning language, and crafting a social identity. In this way, confronting difference leads our group, in Davies and Harre's (1990) terms, to producing "a diversity of selves—the fleeting panorama of Meadian 'me's' conjured up in the course of conversational interactions" (p. 47) and, in so doing, to questioning and complicating taken-for-granted beliefs and values.

Of course, this does not happen to us at each meeting or with each book. Not everything we read challenges us this way—or, perhaps, we read potentially challenging materials with more or less openness or vulnerability depending on other circumstances in our lives. There is much that literary theorists and educators do not yet understand about the transactions that occur in reading multicultural literature. Why, for example, do we sometimes move from assuming family resemblance between our experiences and the author's to constructing what Davidson (1986) calls "passing theories" that enable us to both to locate and understand difference as well as to communicate with another across it (Davidson, paraphrased in Dasenbrock, 1992, p. 41)? On some occasions such as our meeting tonight, members of the Future Teachers' Autobiography Club appear to reach by means of our discussion, a place where, in Dasenbrock's (1992) words,

> we assume similarity but inevitably encounter difference. The encounter with difference, however, is productive, not frustrating, because it causes a change in the interpretive system of the interpreter. (p. 41)

Rodriguez is U.S.-born, Mexican American, and male. His narrative is deceptively ordinary. Richard could be a child in one of our classrooms. Yet his persona as a Hispanic intellectual critical of liberal educational practice and troubled by unresolved identity issues is hard for us to embrace. His rejection of bilingual education and affirmative action occasions great discomfort and confusion among the club members. For example, Julie wonders about what appear to be internal contradictions within Rodriguez's position in his own narrative:

> He said he would have liked to have heard them [his elementary school teachers] address him in Spanish. But later he is so against bilingual education. (Meeting Transcript, 3/25/93)

Marcia confronts his position adding emphatically,

> I disagree with his whole stance on bilingual education because I think that it is a good thing and I think that if we go back to the loss he had . . . I think that kids can learn and grow and perhaps find a public voice but, with bilingual education, still have that close, intimate feeling. (Meeting Transcript, 3/25/93)

Still, Marcia's firmly stated position, framed as a policy, introduces problems as well. Participants wonder, for example, if implicit in having English serve as the public language of adulthood, the intimacy of a family's language and home culture is affronted. Is a mixed message given to students in a situation where their home language, although "honored and preserved" is not part of the language of public commerce and learning? Is language isomorphic with culture? Do all language-minority families value the same experiences for their children?

Rodriguez's narrative further complicates our understanding of the catchphrase, "cultural diversity," by interlacing it with race and socioeconomic class—issues we have tended to skirt on previous evenings. His autobiography lingers, for example, on his obsession with his own skin color and describes his discovery that African American students suffer quite different inequities than members of his ethnic group. He also scrutinizes the economic and educational inequalities within his own ethnic group, stressing that his family's middle class status was an important factor enabling him and his siblings to learn despite the English-only context of their parochial school. He argues from this experience that reform should be primarily economic rather than exclusively linguistic or cultural.

## TAKING A POET'S SPECTATOR STANCE

Despite, or perhaps in virtue of, our disagreements with Rodriguez we are pushed to rethink our ideas about culture. The narrative responses we make to this task are like Britton's (1982) definition of literary, or "poetic," texts. They are not retellings of what we already know or believe or have experienced but are extensions, new constructions made out of our own and others' words and actions and problems. These narratives introduce dramatic action and conflict. We create the drama and orchestrate the action in and through the characters we include and the situations in which we place them. As such, we tell stories from a "spectator" stance, standing outside the action, framing and reframing moral positions on the narrative in our construction of its problem, complicating action, characters, and conclusion. Of this stance, Britton (1982) says,

> a major aspects of the spectator's response to the events he witnesses will be a concern for the people involved and an interest in the way they react, but there is likely to be present also an interest in and evaluation of the pattern events take with a sense that what is happening here might one day happen to him. (p. 153)

As will be seen later, as participants narrate experiences of schooling and identity from the literary stance of a spectator, they investigate aspects of the cultural experience typically framed out of view.

To review our methods, described in chapter 5, Julie and I analyzed the book club meetings for "narrative episodes. "We listened to tapes of the meetings together and coded the transcript of our meeting identifying sequences within which a speaker (or several speakers) rendered a full or partial narrative within the context of the ongoing club conversation. We defined an episode as either an extended turn or connected set of turns. Narratives, either full-blown or "kernel," were accounts of problems, with subsequent actions and consequences. Tracking discussion of culture in these narratives, we noted participants offering individual or jointly constructed accounts of culture as a process of identification transformed over time and in light of social, political, and economic circumstances.

We look at oral personal narrative in terms of its situated nature as well as its text structure. Telling a story is a sociolinguistic performance and, as such, it is about more than its plot. It is profoundly about its teller and its listeners, especially when it is offered in face-to-face conversation. The narratives we identified exhibit many of the features of oral personal narrative as it has been analyzed in folklorists' studies of story telling as both a formal performance and spontaneous personal narratives arising in ordinary conversation (e.g., Bauman, 1986; Hymes, 1981; Labov, 1972; Stahl, 1985).

Personal narratives take ordinary life events and make them "tellable" by giving them dramatic content and structure. Traditionally, this is done by recounting events involving an agent, action(s), object(s), and outcome. However, storytellers sometimes replace the action orientation of narrative with self-revelation. A narrative can reveal inner conflict or an inner mental state or emotional landscape rather than a snapshot of a narrator acting on the environment or other people to solve a problem or resolve a crisis. As dramatic creations, narratives are not literal (and therefore factual) recounting of events or experiences. Labov (1972) argues that even when they arise informally within ordinary conversation, personal narratives have the quality of performances. As such, listeners appear to honor their structure and do not readily dispute them in terms of their factual content (Tannen, 1989). Although the narratives that occur informally within conversation cannot, in fact, be "read" out of the context of that situation, their structural features enable us to isolate them for some analytic purposes. Here we examine a set of such narratives by focusing on their thematic content, narrative structure, and shifting voice. As part and parcel of their dramatic nature, folklorists describe personal narratives as analyzable into the following components:

- Abstract: What was this about?
- Orientation: Who, what, where, when?
- Complication(s): Then what happened?
- Evaluation(s): So what?
- Result or resolution: What finally happened?
- Denouement or coda: Tying back to present conversation situation.

Additionally, storytellers sometimes replace the action orientation of narrative with self-revelation—a narrative can reveal inner conflict or an inner mental state or emotional landscape rather than a snapshot of a narrator acting on the environment or other people to solve a problem or resolve a crisis. In both cases, however, these stories are dramatic. They reveal the narrator as he or she wants others to know him or her, and mobilize others in the story to serve that purpose. In so doing, they have moral or evaluative force. It is in their introduction of dramatic content (especially via conflict internal or external to the narrator) and framing of moral problems that we find the book club members' personal narratives approaching the idea of culture as lived, dynamic, and reinvented by people across time, generations, and experience. When this occurs, narratives foreground learning and the negotiation of identity. These are explored as processes that are not natural, trouble-free, and invisible, but deeply social and thus subject to conflict and change across settings, situations, participants, and power relationships (Soliday, 1994).

Analyzing the conversation that took place on the night we discussed *Hunger of Memory*, Julie and I identified and gave titles to nine narrative episodes in which speakers presented dramatic content to make a claim, raise a question, or pose a problem related to pupil cultural identity and the experience of schooling (see the appendix for examples). As such, these narratives were thematically linked and responsive to issues raised by Rodriguez—especially those epitomized in his idea of the "scholarship boy." Each of the nine narratives we analyzed draws on the speaker's own experience of coming of age or learning to teach to explore the complexities of identity, diversity, and schooling. Marcia's brief narrative, for example, "The Boys in Detroit," exemplifies the way the nine narratives open up examination of educational dilemmas in virtue of an expanded idea of culture. In it, she attempts to explain to her father the plight of young African American males in Detroit as they go to school. She says,

I talk to my dad about this. I am thinking, what if you are an inner city Detroit sixteen-year-old Black male and you want to succeed, want to learn, want to succeed in education to get out of poverty. I guess this is kind of a common thing, but it kind of hit me like a lightening bolt. If I choose one thing that I want, I'm going to be hurt. If I choose the other thing that I want to be: I want to be intimate, I want to live like I have always lived, to enjoy my culture and other things I enjoy in life, I won't have this. It is one or the other. You are isolated. (Meeting Transcript, 3/25/93)

"The Boys in Detroit" was discussed earlier in this book as a kernel narrative reflecting and reinforcing the default mode in our thinking about culture. Its structure and content echo the scholarship boy trope and, at face value, it is another rendition of that cultural meta narrative. However, extended contact with talk and text affords opportunities to revisit our stories. When we look again and more closely at Marcia's narrative, we see some educative possibilities for inquiry and retelling. "The Boys in Detroit" illustrates three general features of the inquiry-oriented narratives we studied. First, it offers a site for the speaker to try out "teaching selves," versions of the teacher she might like to be or become (P. Conway, 1998; Harris, 1995; Nias, 1989). Note, for example, that Marcia casts herself in the role of enlightening her father, presumably less knowledgeable or tolerant of diversity than she. In the reported talk with her father, what Tannen (1989) calls "constructed dialogue," Marcia discovers ("it kind of hit me like a lightening bolt") one powerful rendition of the boys' dilemma that might be of importance to his teacher.

Second, Marcia's narrative embeds multiple voices and perspectives. Note, for example, that there are two protagonists in "The Boys from Detroit." Marcia is the ostensive protagonist telling the story of her conversation with her father. However, the other protagonist in the story is the "inner-city Detroit 16-year-old-Black male" who is faced with the dilemma of losing his private identity in order to attain school success and a public identity therein. This framing closely parallels Rodriguez's narrative structure and the theme of alienation raised in his image of the scholarship boy. In a variation on Rodriguez's shift from referring to his own experience in the first and third person, Marcia refers both to her own and another's experience with the personal pronoun. She strays from a direct matching of the personal pronoun to her own experience, at first referring to her own actions and mental state with the word "I" ("I talk to my dad about this." "I am thinking. . . ." "I guess this is a kind of common thing"), and later animating the boys in Detroit in personal terms as well ("If I choose one thing that I want, I'm going to be hurt").

Following Goffman's (1974) concept of "footing," the narrative thus repositions the narrator in relationship to her subject matter and its listeners by introducing—in Marcia's voice—the position of other speakers not co-present. With this shift in footing, Marcia opens herself and her listeners to another person's experience and the possibility that more is at issue and at stake for the boys than might be immediately apparent to White, middle-class people like Marcia or her father.

A third important feature of Marcia's vignette is that, unlike many oral personal narratives told in this club and elsewhere, hers does not offer a clear moral or easy resolution. As Fig. 6. 1 illustrates, if we map tradi-

---

**FIG. 6.1**   *Narrative Structure of "The Boys in Detroit"*

---

**Abstract:**
*what is this about?*
I talk to my dad about this.

**Orientation:**
*who, what where, when?*
I am thinking, what if you were an inner-city Detroit, 16-year-old Black male, and you want to succeed, want to learn, want to succeed in education to get out of poverty.

**Evaluation(s):**
*so what?*
I guess this is a kind of common thing, but it know of hit me like a lightening bolt,

**Complications(s):**
*then what happened?*
if I choose one thing that I want, I'm going to be hurt. If I choose the other thing that I want to be: I want to be intimate, I want to live like I have always lived, to enjoy my culture and the things I enjoy in life, I won't have this.

**Result/Resolution:**
*what finally happened?*
It is one or the other. You are isolated

tional categories for narrative structure onto her vignette, we find that the narrative's "resolution" is actually a dilemma framed in terse declaratives ("It is one or the other. You are isolated. "). The dilemma prompts difficult questions: How is the teenager to decide? Why is the situation experienced this way? What could be changed to make it less alienating? This vignette illustrates the general tendency for book club participants' cultural narratives increasingly to explore potential aspects of their own identities as teachers and citizens; articulate multiple perspectives on the themes raised in the books under discussion; and raise difficult questions about culture, schooling, and identity. It is to the narrative mechanisms of such inquiry that we now turn.

## EXPANDING OUR DEFINITION OF CULTURE

We were surprised to find in the set of nine narrative episodes analyzed that their themes greatly expanded and diversified the group's working definitions of both culture and identity. Instead of identity deriving from a set of traditions, practices, and beliefs narrowly circumscribed and passed on in the families of particular ethnic or racial groups, we see evidence in themes of participants' narratives of emerging complexity. Prompted by Rodriguez's images of the public and the private, the alienation a learner can experience by making choices about his or her cultural identity, and his or her criticisms' of the solutions we take for granted as liberal educators, narrators unpack a series of questions or dilemmas exploring four themes:

1.  The affective dimensions of cultural change—especially the feeling of loss that accompanies a person's move from primary socialization in the family to learning secondary discourses within formal schooling.
2.  Tthe experience of gender as part of individual and cultural change—especially participants' recognition that, in some cases, the pursuit of formal education can cause conflict of identity for girls and women similar to those Rodriguez describes around his Mexican American identity and learning in a second languages.
3.  Peer culture—especially the idea that "culture" is not a monolithic phenomenon isolated and passed on within families but can be learned in other arenas to forge social identities with other affiliates such as friends or age peers.
4.  Resistance—like peer culture, this phenomenon is examined in the narratives as participants explore the idea of volition as it relates to culture, the possibility

that individuals may or may not appropriate the cultural practices of the group in which they find themselves for reasons related to their local identity needs and goals and also to the broader social, political, and historical contexts in which they find themselves.

While the full text of a sample set of these narratives is included in the appendix, Table 6.1 summarizes the thematic content of the nine narratives described here.[1] In the table, we title each narrative episode to highlight the topic with which it deals. We also group the nine into four clusters according to the aspect of culture and identity they dramatize. In the first set, Peggy and Misty narrate their discovery, on returning home from college, that intimacy with their parents has been undermined. For Peggy, the issue is mismatch between her own educational aspirations and attainments and those of her noncollege-educated father. This mismatch makes it difficult for Peggy to feel at home with her family or communicate with them about much of her school life.

For Misty, whose father is a high school teacher, the mismatch underlying her narrative is not so much educational as social and geographic. Living at some distance from her family and responsible for her own daily living and moral decisions, she feels a shift from the former intimacy of her family to a more impersonal way of communicating. There are aspects of her life she cannot express to them, and they cannot know. Misty is surprised to realize that this experience can transcend language code differences. She speculates that she shares this experience with Rodriguez despite the fact that she has negotiated the passage from home to school without a change in language code. Following on her vignette, Peggy and Julie offer a coda posing the following dilemma shared with Rodriguez:

> **Peggy:** We say that we have changed a lot . . . and we are not as comfortable with our parents or relate as well because of college.
>
> **Julie:** But we didn't change our language.
>
> **Peggy:** Right, we didn't change our language at all . . . but we changed anyway. And we would never say, I mean, I don't think many would propose maybe we shouldn't go to college.

---

[1] See the appendix for the full text of sample narratives.

**TABLE 6.1**  *Narratives Told in Response to* Hunger of Memory *and Their Relation to an Expanded Understanding of Culture, Diversity, and Education*

| Themes | Narrative episodes | Issues/Questions |
|---|---|---|
| Loss and cultural change | "Peggy at college" "Misty at college" | Acquiring new cultural discourses by going to school—Is this only when learning a new language? The experience of loss and transformation in the transition from home to school—What is defined as success and what does it gain and cost the individual? the group? |
| Gender and cultural identity | "Marcia in elementary school" "Rusha and Waffa" | How does gender relate to other aspects of cultural experience? Is home culture independent of/irrelevant to school culture? Are we/ should we be cultural relativists in our teaching practice? |
| Peer culture | "Peggy at camp" "Acting Black" | What is peer culture? How is cultural identity changed by intergroup contact? Do cultures change across generations and with contact? |
| Resistance | "La Toya's cut-downs" "Cole's mom" "The Boys in Detroit" | Why do people appropriate or resist aspects of the culture in which they find themselves? How is resistance related to identity? |

In the second set of narratives, the theme shifts to culturally patterned assumptions about gender and its relationship to intellectual identity. Although not explicitly raised in Rodriguez's book, gender is a characteristic around which club members narrate their own recollected experiences of violating normative expectations of their family or peer group similar to Richard's experience of going to school and becoming a high achiever. Marcia talks of her very mixed feelings about being a high achieving youngster and how difficult it was for her to accept the teacher's accolades. As a girl, she wanted the acceptance of boys and saw high achievement and "standing out" in school as antithetical to a feminine identity. Now a young woman, the issue continues to plague her as she thinks about how to reconcile her desire for a rich intellectual life with her equivalent desire for a male partner.

Misty speaks from her vantage point as a student teacher. She narrates the experiences of two young female Arabic students in her fourth-grade class—one who appears to have embraced American norms for female assertiveness and one whose family encourages her to behave in more traditional, and to Misty more subdued, Arabic ways. Of significance in comparing the girls' experiences are the parents' plans either to remain in the United States after completing their work at the university or to return to Saudi Arabia. Misty's example highlights both the transformative influence of public education as well as a person or group's power to resist socialization into new norms on the basis of previously held beliefs and sense of identity. These narratives also introduce gender as a crosscutting issue in education and in the negotiation of cultural identity. Her narrative suggests, as research by di Leonardo (1984) and Sarroub (2000) has also found, that over time and cultural contact, gender identity like ethnic identity is often transformed and reinvented. Just as Richard's identity as a Mexican American is different from that of his parents, so the young women realize that participation in public education can be transformative of gender identity—for the young Arabic girls and for themselves.

A third cluster of narratives examines the theme of peer culture in school as well as transformations in cultural experience due to intercultural contact. Peggy tells of being the only White counselor at a summer camp near Detroit and finding herself inclined to learn new ways and styles of interacting in order to get along with her African American counselor colleagues. In contrast, Julie tells of an African-American high school friend who grew up with her in the affluent suburbs and then left to attend an urban university. When he came home from college for Christmas vacation, she was struck by how he had changed and had begun to "act Black." These stories, like those concerning gender identity, raise for the group the idea that people differentially appropriate or reject aspects of communication style that might be thought of as "cultural" and that these decisions are related in part to other features of identity such as situational context, institutional role, and peer groups.

The final cluster of narratives further develops affective issues related to cultural identity. They also illustrate that race or first language might not be the only determinant of access to schooling. "Cole's Mom" is the story of a White family in which the youngster is struggling to learn to read, but the mother is resistant to participation in his schooling because she is herself marginally literate. An economically disadvantaged single parent, the mother did not complete formal education and the story opens speculation about the sources of her resistance to Cole's teachers. This narrative resonates with Rodriguez's observation that educational inequality and lack of access to learning is a broad social problem not restricted to members of particular racial or ethnic or linguistic groups, but spanning all groups and highly related to economic status.

Finally, in "La Toya's Cut-Downs," Julie returns to an examination of the behavior of her student whose verbalizations at peers and teachers have troubled her so greatly. Although her earlier recounting of La Toya's cut-downs located responsibility for the behavior in her family ("they get it at home"), this vignette revisits La Toya after considerable discussion of the issues raised by Rodriguez's book. As Julie and Peggy tell the story together now, they raise the possibility that the student resists school-appropriate behavior out of fear of loss of a sense of herself ("I think she is afraid to say to me . . . I mean she wanted to defend her way."). In addition, Peggy closes with an expanded array of experiences at play for La Toya at home, in school, and among peers. All of these might be considered "cultural," and Peggy reflects on them as offering sets of norms and values. Acknowledging the possibility that they are not aligned with one another, she finds in La Toya's case that cultural conflict forces difficult decisions on the student. This analysis situates identity within normative social contexts and, while it might be criticized for overdrawing the degree to which these contexts are both normative and isolated from one another, it widens considerably the lens through which we can view La Toya and reasonably interpret both her behavior and her perspective.

Tracking discussion of culture in narrative response to autobiographical text, we find book club talk about culture, especially the stories told in conversation, to be considerably richer than we might have expected given extant research on beginning teachers' understandings of the idea of cultural diversity. In response to *Hunger of Memory*, participants narrate complex accounts of culture as a complex process of identification transformed over time and in light of social, political, and economic circumstances. That process is made more difficult in the face of social and economic inequality. And it is still more difficult in the face of race and racism—topics that inevitably arise as club members tell stories in response to Rodriguez's book.

The narrative responses to Rodriguez's book weave a richly detailed tapestry in which participants represent the concepts of "culture" and "identity" as more complex in nature, more risky in content, and more interesting in educational possibility than they might without benefit of conversation and compelling literature. In the next two chapters we continue our look at the book club's examination of culture—especially as it is related in the United States to social class and race. To do this we analyze a difficult conversation that took place on the evening we gathered to talk about Maya Angelou's first autobiographical book, *I Know Why the Caged Bird Sings*.

# CHAPTER 7

# Transformative Genres

In an essay titled "Con Artists and Storytellers," Lionnet (1989) says that in reluctantly writing the first book in what would become a multivolume autobiography, Maya Angelou was not attempting to reveal her "personal affairs" or her "inner soul." To support her assertion, Lionnet cites a passage from *I Know Why the Caged Bird Sings* in which Maya describes her grandmother, Momma's, counsel on how to use language as follows:

> Knowing Momma, I knew I never knew Momma. Her African-bush secretiveness and suspiciousness had been compounded by slavery and confirmed by centuries of promises made and promises broken. We have a saying among Black Americans, which describes Momma's caution. "If you ask a Negro where he's been, he'll tell you where he's going." To understand this important information, it is necessary to know who uses this *tactic* and on whom it works. If an *unaware person* is told a part of the truth (it is imperative that the answer embody truth), he is satisfied that his query has been answered. If an *aware person* (*one who himself uses the stratagem*) is given an answer which is truthful but bears only slightly if at all on the question, he knows that the information he seeks is of a private nature and will not be handed to him willingly. Thus direct denial, lying and the revelation of personal affairs are avoided. (Angelou, 1970, pp. 164–165, cited in Lionnet, 1989, p. 131, italics added by Lionnet)

Following Momma's description, Lionnet argues that when Angelou was encouraged by a commercial publisher to write her life "as literature," she crafted a response culturally appropriate to her African-American upbringing. Angelou responded to the request for an autobiography not by imitating the genre Euro-American editors and readers expected, but by fictionalizing her life with two different audiences (or interlocutors) in mind. Although for an African American audience this genre may serve, in the tradition of 19th-century slave narratives, to testify to a shared experience, for its Euro-American audience, Lionnet suggests a different purpose, that of critiquing mainstream Euro-American institutions and their genres. Lionnet (1989) writes that

> because the autobiographical project was a response to external pressures, it is in
> many ways directed to a white audience, but at the same time, it succeeds in gestur-
> ing toward the black community, which shares a long tradition among oppressed
> peoples of understanding duplicitous uses of language for survival. (p. 130)

Lionnet argues that Angelou's autobiographical writing used language, not referentially to express the literal details of her coming of age experiences, but figuratively to craft vignettes allegorically exposing good and evil from her point of view. In telling her life story as a series of fictionalized vignettes, Angelou employed folk traditions of African-American oral narrative, thus challenging conventional assumptions of a mostly White mainstream audience that autobiography be presented as if it were factual. Expecting the genre to bear the weight of factual accounting alienates the writer from both the moral force of her experiences and the relationship she hopes to forge with her readers. In contrast, the folk tradition in which Angelou participates enables her to build narrative connections with her own life experiences and her readers or listeners. Moreover, Angelou was in the vanguard among U.S. writers from relatively disempowered ethnic groups in crafting of autobiography what Lionnet calls "metissage," or

> A complex weave of linguistic, racial, and gendered selves....describing the
> braided weave of multiple and composite identities that may intentionally be
> drawn from experience in acts of self authorization. It is a way of acting and
> reflecting upon multiplicity without essentializing any aspect. (Lionnet, 1989, p.
> 14; also cited in Zuss, 1997, p. 166)

This is a powerful rhetorical move within contemporary autobiography. It confronts the reader with text violating conventional assumptions about autobiography's truthfullness or factuality. It also offers portrayals of authors and other characters in their stories that are multifaceted, difficult to pin down or stereotype. In these ways, contemporary autobiographies, especially by authors from groups traditionally not offered access to the genre, confront readers with a text that bears a "double reading" and limit readers' assumptions of essential categories such as gender, ethnicity, race, social class, and the like (Zuss, 1997). They also serve to heighten readers' attention to the idea of "masking" by less powerful persons in the presence of more powerful ones. This is a theme that occurs in other works by Angelou, including a poem she adapted from Paul Laurence Dunbar's poem, "We Wear the Mask."

The vignettes comprising the text of *Caged Bird* have a folkloric texture. They paint people, places, and events in bold strokes, yet they appear also to mask powerful, unexpressed feeling of anger, pain, and fear. In a move that surprises the book club readers, Maya Angelou does not report her experiences chronologically, in a plotlike chain of events. Nor does she offer relentless detail. Instead, she sketches them episodically as if recalling, reconstructing, and retelling them from childhood and a child's point of view. They have the quality of fantasy, and it was common for both Future Teachers' Autobiography Club members and students in my subsequent master's course to raise the question, on encountering Angelou's books, "Is it true?"

The following example illustrates. It comes from the book club discussion of experienced teachers in the course, "Culture, Literacy, and Autobiography." Here, experienced teachers talk about the same book read by the future teachers. This exchange, identified by Glazier (1997) in her analyses of teachers' conversation in that course, underscores the engaging yet disarming effect of Angelou's narrative style and content on an audience of middle-class, White, female teacher-readers:

**Hannah:** I'm like . . . She did *not* spend a month in a car.

**Kate:** I get such a kick out of how she would condense major feelings into one line . . . or one sentence . . . I mean you are talking about something that would take a book to write.

**Bonnie:** Just so much of this, I mean, gosh, most of this book is so painful but, you know, you look back and its almost funny some of the stuff!

**Hannah:** Chasing the preacher. Like I was just laughing hysterically during that part. It was *so funny*. I mean, and its *not funny*, because, I mean, like that woman was forever, for whatever reason, just overtaken (Class Transcript, 9/25/95; italics note speaker emphasis).

The autobiography's vignettes are incredible. Like poetry, they are compressed. Although brief, they are intense and emotionally powerful. They are funny; they are tragic. We cannot dismiss them. The poetic, allegorical shaping of Angelou's vignettes permits her to draw her Euro-American readers into intimate contact with her while at the same time mounting powerful criticisms of the dominant institutions they value and take for granted. With this in mind, it is interesting to consider the Future Teachers' Autobiography Clubs' response to Angelou's book, *I Know Why the Caged Bird Sings*. This is a book from which one or two vignettes are often excerpted to be read in courses dealing with multicultural education. Yet the power of reading the book in its entirety is that what are at first glance "true stories" of events that happened to Maya become part of a complex tapestry of experience that imaginatively creates lived experience out of bits and pieces of narrative, both recollected and invented.

## MAYA'S GRADUATION

Reading *I Know Why the Caged Bird Sings* in its entirety and as part of her "White audience," it is not surprising that the book's vignettes unsettled us and became the source of much heated discussion. Angelou's book did not permit us smooth or comfortable categorization of the author as "culturally different" from ourselves. Her text confronted us in rapid-fire succession with a series of disturbing personal accounts having to do with race and with our implication in the racism that she portrays. We were not able to read them at arm's length or with a benign appreciation for the trials and tribulations of the author's life because we are implicated in sustaining the conditions of inequality she describes.

The self-examination that Angelou's autobiographical vignettes prompted had implications for what we discussed and how we discussed it. It is perhaps no coincidence, for example, that on the night we discussed *Caged Bird* we engaged most directly in argument over issues of educational equity. We discovered that various members of our own group had experienced the privileges of public education differently and held different beliefs about access to education. These differences dominated our talk as the club became, not just a place for talking how "people from other cultures" differed from ourselves, but a laboratory for exposing and exploring our own differences as well and attempting the difficult work of negotiating common ground in the face of difference. This dangerous ground was entered as a part of our group's examination of race and racism as aspects of culture and diversity in the United States.

The club's conflict on this night centered on schooling not as a social and economic system in which power, privilege and resources for learning are unevenly distributed. Of central importance in our discussion was a vignette in Angelou's autobiography recounting her graduation from grammar school. Written with an arc-like structure from anticipation to triumph to despair, Angelou begins her narrative by describing her rising anticipation of the glory that is to come with her graduation from grammar school. Angelou (1969) says,

> The children of Stamps trembled visibly with anticipation. Some adults were excited, too, but to be certain the whole young population had come down with graduation epidemic. Large classes were graduating from both the grammar school and the high school. Even those who were years removed from their own day of glorious release were anxious to help with the preparations as a kind of dry run. . . . But the graduating classes themselves were the nobility. (p. 142)

Noblest among nobles, we learn that Angelou has been awarded first place in her class based on her academic work. She tells of her plans for the day—what she will wear, how she will comb her hair, how the prospect of graduating as leader of her class is itself transforming her. Finally, after weeks of preparation, the day arrives, and Angelou describes its dawning with an almost religious reverence, suggesting its resurrectionlike quality:

> I hoped the memory of that morning would never leave me. Sunlight was itself still young and the day had none of the insistence maturity would bring it in a few hours. In my robe and barefoot in the backyard, under cover of going to see about my new beans, I gave myself up to the gentle warmth and thanked God that no matter what evil I had done in my life He allowed me to see this day. (p. 147)

To this point, Angelou has created a scene with which all of us could identify. We, too, had graduated and felt pride and transformation in that accomplishment. In fact, to read these passages as intending teachers might underscore our valuing of education and our belief in the institution of schooling and the power of its rituals. However, Angelou foreshadows difficult things to come in her mention of "the insistence maturity would bring in a few hours." As we read on, she describes the long-awaited grad-uation ceremony with its quick dismantling of her joy and optimism. As Maya's principal introduces Mr. Donleavy, a White school district admin-istrator, a pall descends on both Maya's spirits and the entire event of graduation. Coming from a distance to "speak and run," Donleavy's remarks center on the improvements being made to the schools of more affluent White students and on the outstanding athleticism of the African-American boys in Maya's school, particularly in football and basketball. Maya tells us that, although the students at Central School were getting new books and laboratory equipment,

> Donleavy was running for election, and assured our parents that if he won we could count on having the only colored paved playing field in that part of Arkansas. Also—he never looked up to acknowledge the grunts of acceptance—also, we were bound to get some new equipment for the home economics build-ing and workshop. (p. 153)

Maya, who loves books, is hurt and angered by his remarks, not only for what they say about the distribution of resources, but for their crip-pling expression of the dominant community's expectations of her and her class. She uses the word "colored" to underscore his disrespect and cate-gorical thinking about the students in her school, and he fails to acknowl-edge the audience response. For its part, the audience "grunts" its acceptance, a hardly ringing endorsement for his promise and a response that makes the audience seem demoralized. Perhaps their silence is the only apt form of resistance in this situation. Juxtaposing her own consid-erable academic accomplishments with blacktop and basketball, Angelou moves toward the completion of her narrative with its arc falling in despair and betrayal as follows:

> Graduation, the hush-hush magic time of frills and gifts and congratulations and diplomas, was finished for me before my name was called. The accomplishment was nothing. The meticulous maps, drawn in three colors of ink, learning and spelling decassyllabic words, memorizing the whole of *The Rape of Lucrece*—it was for nothing. Donleavy had exposed us. We were maids and farmers, handy-men and washerwomen, and anything higher that we aspired to was farcical and presumptuous. (p. 152)

But, as is characteristic of her stories, Angelou offers a coda that reverses things. Before long, Donleavy is gone, and silence is replace by singing, not the programmed material, but a student led, spontaneous rendition of "Lift Every Voice and Sing." Maya tells us,

> We were on top again. As always, again. We survived. The depths had been icy
> and dark, bu now a bright sun spoke to our souls. I was no longer simply a member of the proud graduating class of 1940; I was a proud member of the wonderful, beautiful Negro race (p. 156).

## FICTIONALIZING SELF

This vignette is characteristic of many of those comprising the autobiography. The book is a collection of loosely chronological and personal vignettes of her youth in Stamps and later in California. As such, it contains, not a singular, monolithic plot of her coming of age, but a set of briefer accounts. They seem deceptively simple and sketchy. But on closer examination they reveal that word choice, event structure, character, and setting are crafted to give the stories moral force. As in a morality play, the characters introduced embody particular moral and political forces and points of view. Some, like Momma, reappear throughout the book and carry leitmotifs, repeated as these characters reappear, and are gradually developed. Others, like Donleavy, appear briefly, almost as caricatures standing for institutions, groups, and practices to which Angelou wants to draw critical attention.

Similarly some settings, like Momma's store in Stamps, recur and become familiar to the reader as places where Maya's evolving point of view is rooted. Others, like the office of the dentist who refuses treatment to Maya and her grandmother, are visited memorably, but only once. Angelou selects the events to be reported and develops their structure to press moral points. Yet through all this artistry, her vignettes are eminently "tellable" and seem much like the oral stories many of us—regardless of racial or cultural background—have heard told and retold by members of our own families.

Angelou's autobiographical vignettes prefigure and provoke personal narratives told by members of the book club. Our oral narratives, like her written ones, were offered in sequences or rounds accumulating to make a larger statement about what a person (or coalition of persons) in the group believes. As such, they were not literal transcriptions of experience but constructions or performances crafted to represent what speakers believe and wish others to believe about what they have experienced. We select from the ordinary stream of life events "worth telling about." We narrate some of these experiences for their power to express deeply held beliefs and values, particularly as they dramatize moments when those beliefs and values are challenged by people (and institutions) who hold other points of view and have the power to threaten our emerging sense of our self and the world (Soliday, 1994).

Studying and transacting in personal narrative, we discover that it is unhelpful and distorting to impose on autobiography dualisms such as fact versus fiction or personal versus social. Autobiography is a slippery genre for both literary theorists and social scientists precisely because it resists neat categorizing and thereby opens the entire question of the categorize-ability of into genres. Yet, literary critic Stone (1981) observes that although autobiography thus frustrates at least some academics and their efforts to analyze it and fix its properties, it is a powerful genre with which lay readers are exceedingly comfortable. Perhaps this is because autobiography asks them to read, as they tend both to speak and listen, making interpretations of social meaning and personal identity within and by means of the telling of experience. Of this Stone says,

> The autobiographer aims to recreate the self-in-its world, not by literal reproduction of remembered facts (a boring as well as impossible achievement), but by patterning the past into a present and symbolic truth. . . . Writers and readers form a "pact" or contractual community. They commonly agree that the language of autobiography points both *outwards* the world of the remembered experience and *inward* to a reflective consciousness. Thus like all narratives—including, of course, histories—autobiography is simultaneously fact and fiction. (pp. 6–7)

Here, we take a close look at conversation within the meeting of the book club during which we discussed Angelou's book. This discussion was noteworthy to us because within it, club members engaged in a complex interaction that included both moments of intense conflict and periods of consensus building. Angelou's material prompted participants to confront in her text as well as in their own experiences the idea that difference among students is not necessarily a benign reality. Angelou's vignettes force consideration of race and inequality within American institutions such as public schools. As Euro-American educators, those of us gathered to discuss her book were implicated in Angelou's critique. It would not be easy for us to dismiss her graduation story nor would it be easy for us to frame responses to it.

## TALKING ABOUT *CAGED BIRD*

The Future Teachers' Autobiography Club met to discuss *Caged Bird* on January 21, 1993. In addition to myself as host, all six of the other members were in attendance. This was the club's second monthly meeting and the first since winter break. Now working full time in their student teaching sites, the members were eager to see one another after a long separation. Interest in Angelou's book was high because she had recently delivered a poem at President Clinton's inauguration, and her work and life were therefore widely reported in newspapers and on television.

Conversation on this night did not unfold as a unitary or ritualized performance. Instead, it was a dancelike ensemble in which participants negotiated shifts in topic and ways of speaking, moving back and forth from doubting to believing, from conflict to consensus. The meeting begins and ends, for example, with transitional talk we call "topic finding" and "concluding." Talk during these phases links this evening's conversation with our conversations at other club meetings (both retrospectively and prospectively). It also moves participants from life and events outside the club to the evening's informal agenda and back again.

Looking at talk within the body of the meeting, Julie and I identified two periods when participants exchanged ideas about the evening's published autobiography and their own lives. These periods would correspond to "genres" in Burbules' model, but we call them "phases" in order to capture their dynamic, negotiated quality. We labeled them "debate" and "joint inquiry." Our analysis illustrates that each phase involves club members in different ways of participating and different kinds of intellectual work. Each phase also mobilizes narrative knowledge (about the text in common, other texts, or participants' lives) in different ways. Helping the group sustain coherent conversation across these two phases are transitions in which changes in the nature and direction of talk are negotiated. We labeled these "reframing" and "repair."

The work of Burbules (1993) on dialogue in teaching was helpful to us in this analysis. As the adaptation of Burbules' ideas in Table 7.1 illustrates, "dialogue" can be thought of as the superordinate category of educational talk encompassing various types or "genres" such as debate, conversation, inquiry and instruction. These genres engage participants with knowledge and with one another in different ways. Educational dialogues may very in nature and purpose. They may be seeking consensus and problem solving. Alternately, they articulate different ways of thinking about a complex problem where no consensus is sought or even possible. They may also be

**TABLE 7.1**   *Genres of Dialogue in Education*

| Function | Convergent | Divergent |
|---|---|---|
| Inclusive "believing" | Consensus-oriented inquiry | Conversation |
| Critical "doubting" | Instruction | Debate |

*Note. Adapted from Burbules (1993) and Florio-Ruane and de Tar (1995).*

oriented toward the acceptance of others' ideas (or "believing") or their refutation (or "doubting"). Burbules (1993) uses the term *dialogue* in a generic sense and specifies *conversation* as one genre of dialogue. In my writing, I tend to use the term *conversation* as the generic because it is conventionally used that way in sociolinguistics and conversational analysis. The terms *dialogue* and *conversation* are used interchangeably here, but the genre differences articulated by Burbules are dealt with in this chapter.

Burbules draws the contrast between dialogues as "believing" and "doubting" from Peter Elbow, who argues that our Western intellectual tradition inclines us to view skepticism, or doubting, as the primary means of critical thinking. Of this tradition Elbow (1986) says, "we tend to assume that the ability to criticize a claim we disagree with counts as more serious intellectual work than the ability to enter into it and temporarily assent" (p. 258). He finds in his practice as a writing teacher that interpretive response to text (both published and those written by peers) is often impeded by a rush to doubt it. This adversarial response often blocks other ways of experiencing and understanding text and impoverishes talk about it. Therefore, Elbow devised a "game" to be played in his writing classes where students would be required to engage alternatively in "methodological believing" in which "each participant promises to try to believe what the others see in return for the others trying to believe what she sees" (p. 259). Elbow describes the game as follows:

> When a reader is telling what she sees in a text or what happened to her in reading, the writer and the other readers must not just shut up, they must actively try as hard as they can to believe her—to see and experience the text as she does. This may be our only hope of seeing something faint that is actually there which she is good at seeing but the rest of us are ill suited to see. (p. 259)

The idea of "methodological believing" parallels Dewey's concept of "listening" and Mead's examination of social and personal transformation in the dialogue of self and other (Harris, 1995). This sort of listening does not assume a more powerful other tolerating speech different from her own. Instead, it requires the listener to enter into the sense making of the speaker in much the way that ethnographers attempt to understand other cultural perspectives by entering into relationships with native informants. As such, listening—or methodological believing—is a powerful tool for transforming thought that poses challenges and risks to the listener or learner's identity. The next chapter explores this power and risk as it arose in the book club's discussion of race and inequality.

Although Elbow raises "believing" to consciousness as a method and parallels it to "methodological doubting," Burbules suggests that these ways of participating can be present informally as "genres" or alternative styles of participating that participants negotiate as they make their way through educational conversations. In describing these genre differences, Burbules does not suggest that each genre neatly connect to a particular speech event such that either participants or observer can think of one dialogue as an instance of "debate," while another is exclusively "conversation."

Except in the most narrowly circumscribed and formalized talk (e.g., a debating contest, a court of law, or the initiation–reply–evaluation sequence found in some classroom recitations), socially negotiated norms for turn-taking and topic identification are flexible, and within any dialogue one is likely to find (or experience) elements of more than one genre. Burbules suggests that although these genres are distinct and fall into "regular prototypical patterns," in real dialogue they are "combined and overlapping in multiple way" (Burbules, 1993, p. 110). More research is needed to understand how conversants produce and navigate such combinations and overlapping and to discern how these genres manifest themselves in dialogues with explicit educational content and purposes.

## CONVERSATIONAL GENRES

Describing research on the shifting forms and functions of language in conversation, Cazden (1974) notes that "any interaction has two basic dimensions" (p. 62). There is the sequence of utterances that is related to speakers' intentions and ongoing events in which they are related (syntagmatic), and "there are the options selected at particular moments by particular speakers to express those intents" (p. 63), (paradigmatic). She notes that if the referential meaning conveyed is the same, selection of

particular utterances at those points usually carries different social information. Competent communication involves not only participation in and
awareness of syntagmatic sequences, but recognition of a range of possible acceptable expressive options available at particular points in the
sequence and of the social meanings likely to be carried by choice of one
of those options (e.g., playfulness, anger, urgency, etc.).

Although such schemata vary in the degree to which they prespecify
behavior (compare, e.g., the phases of talk and activity in Catholic mass,
ordering at a fast food restaurant, or asking for a date), they are culturally
patterned and enacted by participants who share (or come to share) a definition of situation. Participating in a novel situation like the book club, it
is possible that the members (especially early in the life history of the
group) must come to a negotiated understanding of the overall structure of
the meetings. In doing this, they may superimpose on the meetings
schemata drawn from other, more familiar situations such as school-based
book discussion or dinner conversation in informal, same-gender groups.
It is also likely that they will import into this situation, ways of participating with one another developed in other setting and contexts. Syntagmatic
analysis highlights the structure of conversations in and through time. It
also reveals transitions between segments, often pointing up moments of
discontinuity or disagreement about the definition of the situation, and
making visible the roles of various speakers play in moving the dialogue
along.

In addition to a dialogue's sequential or syntagmatic structure, participants exercise choice of options about how to speak within the phases.
Linguists refer to this as conversation's *paradigmatic dimension*. It is here
that we look to identify the variations in how particular dialogue genres
are actually realized in speech. Although these realizations differ in their
surface manifestations (e.g., if speakers are identifiably engaging in
"debate" or "conversation"), we would predict particular distinctive features in their otherwise novel and creative talk. Knowing how this is
accomplished helps us understand what participants need to know and be
able to do in order to produce and interpret different forms and functions
of dialogue.

As researchers, this way of listening to conversation offers a conceptual frame through which to view the twists and turns of club members'
talk. As teachers, the analysis reveals to us the difficulty as well as the possibility in talk about literature and culture. Analyzing the conversation in
which we also participated, Julie deTar and I took a second, closer look at
the struggle that Julie experienced and reported. In the next chapter we

describe that second look, noting in the paradigmatic and syntagmatic dimensions of participants' talk the warp and woof of a book club—how the thread of conversation about *Caged Bird* is woven. The fabric thus created in our talk about text incorporates difficulty and sociability, conflict and consensus, believing and doubting, discovery and denial.

# CHAPTER **8**

# Difficult Conversations

The meeting opened with talk we call, "topic finding." Although finding a topic occurs in most conversations, it is less prolonged on formal occasions with clear agendas and designated leaders. Topic finding in our club is noteworthy because it offers evidence for this event's negotiated nature. The talk on this night began as participants entered my home and gradually assembled their full complement in my family room. Thus, book talk finding commenced without all members present and did not include me. I remained in the kitchen, preparing the dinner. The conversation had a roaming, spontaneous quality, but it quickly touched on Angelou's book.

## FINDING A TOPIC

People settled in as I put the finishing touches on the meal. Speakers offered various topics—loosely associated to one another—but initially no single topic or leader "took hold." Still, the candidate topics foreshadowed what was to come. They touched on the book—particularly Angelou's account of her graduation from eighth grade in which the White superintendent announced that Maya's school would get a new playground while the school of middle-class, Euro-American students would get new books. This is a vignette that, unbeknownst to me, the six student members had already discussed in an educational foundations course, and recalling it led to brief snatches of talk on associated topics.

Club members mentioned African American students being channeled into sports and cited the film, *Boyz in the Hood*, in which these issues arise. Reviewing the transcript of this talk, high involvement was evidenced by broad participation, with most members speaking. Also characteristic of this period was overlapping, in which one member would initiate her turn before a previous speaker had finished speaking. In addition to overlapping, there was a high degree of repetition of the words of previous speakers. Both overlapping and repetition are characteristic of speakers, especially in informal circumstances, working to create and sustain conversational involvement (Irvine, 1979; Tannen, 1989).

I entered with the last plate of food. Everyone had now been served and was seated in a circle around the coffee table. Misty, making a move toward leadership in topic selection, returned to the topic of Angelou as the members began to eat. She took an extended speaking turn in which she told the group about how she used her reading of the book and Angelou's participation in the inauguration as an occasion to teach her elementary school class about the poet. She was excited about this connection because she erroneously understood the school where Angelou now teaches to be "Lake Forest" (rather than Wake Forest) and said that this school is very near where she grew up. As the following excerpt illustrates, this excited her pupils and added an air of immediacy to their discussion of Maya Angelou.

> **Misty:** I'm like, "at Lake Forest, and that's where my friend goes to school." They're like, "Oh my God." And it got to the point where, I was telling Edward, they were acting like I knew her or something. At that point, I mean, I made it clear that I was just reading her book, but at that point, I didn't almost really even care why they were excited.

> **Susan:** They were.

> **Misty:** I was just glad they were in tune and excited.

**Peggy:** Misty?

**Misty:** Yeah.

**Peggy:** Where are you from?

Thus, began the group's identification of a topic that would concern them for the next phase of the meeting. Peggy questioned Misty at some length and discovered that she comes from Winnetka, Illinois and was a student at New Trier High School. As the following vignette illustrates, this information is of interest to Peggy because New Trier is a wealthy public school profiled in a book she has been reading, Jonathan Kozol's (1991) *Savage Inequalities.*

> **Misty:** OK. Evanston's where Northwestern University is and Evanston is ten minutes maybe even less from my, like . . . the high school . . . from my house. It's probably like New Trier <u>High School</u>[1]
>
> **Peggy:** <u>New Trier</u>
>
> **Misty:** Yeah. That's my high school.
>
> **Susan:** It's in Savage Inequalities?
>
> **Misty:** Oh, it should be, I mean, like the monetary support and the privileges that are there. It's a small college.
>
> **Peggy:** And public.
>
> **Misty:** It's <u>public.</u>
>
> **Peggy:** <u>That's </u>what makes me so angry. I mean I can't even...oh, I'm really angry reading
>
> **Misty:** Well, its just because everybody who lives there has the money to do it.
>
> **Peggy:** And it's really a caste system.

---

[1]Underlining indicates overlapping speech. Italics indicate speaker emphasis.

**Nell:** It's the same thing with Bloomfield Hills and Pontiac. It's all property taxes that pay for it. And the property, you know, the property in Bloomfield Hills is worth a lot more.

**Peggy:** But that's not all and that's what actually I'm learning.

## DOUBTING: THE DEBATE

The previous exchange was different from initial topic-finding talk in that just two speakers—Misty and Peggy—dominated it. Consistent with the informality and high involvement of the topic-finding phase, the speakers punctuated one another's turns, often overlapping each other. However, here they did not repeat one another's words. Instead, they spoke of two sources of information inaccessible to the other participants and also to one another: Misty's high school and Kozol's book. Their talk ushered in Phase 1 or what might be thought of as one "genre" within this conversation. It was a spirited and sometimes heated debate that brought Peggy into conflict with Misty and ultimately with a speaking coalition formed by Misty and Nell.

This phase involved the sustained exploration of one topic and saw turns (and perhaps the conversational leadership to determine topic) concentrated in just a few participants. The exploration of topic occurred in a context of "doubting," with speakers making and refuting assertions based on the authority either of a text (in this case Kozol's book) or their own experience. The one text in common, Angelou's book, was not explicitly referenced here, but the fairness and funding issues her graduation vignette raised remained very much in the foreground of discussion.

The group found its way into a debate about issues of fairness in school finance. There was a complicated mix of text-based and personal knowledge operant in the debate. But because only one member of the group had read the book referred to and because the debate centered around a community described in the book and also the home of one of the club's members, four of the seven members present did not take active roles in the debate. The debate became so fixed on personal experience that participants do not appear by its end to have reached consensus or learned more than they previously knew based on rethinking their own views or hearing what others had to say. Instead, the debate had an escalating quality in which individuals hardened their views into defensive positions.

In this phase of the meeting, two participants (Nell and Misty) supported one point of view in a speaking coalition. They extended and amplified one another's comments in response to the point of view and comments of another speaker (Peggy) with whom they played the "doubting game." O'Connor and Michaels (1993) describe a related phenomenon in teacher-led discussion where teachers "revoice" student comments to help them make knowledge claims and learn means of academic discussion. In the club, participants used revoicing to underscore or show alignment with the comments made by other speakers.

At first this dialogue has a dispassionate "give-and-take" quality. Peggy asks, and Misty offers, factual information about the Winnetka area and the New Trier High School. The talk turns personal however, when Nell, who attended an affluent private school in a Detroit suburb, offers an anecdote in which her own school was presented in a television news program in stark contrast to the impoverished Detroit schools nearby. Again, the contrast is echoed by Misty who compares New Trier with the high school in Evanston, a less affluent city also near Chicago. Both Misty and Nell speak about pride in their high schools and the preparation they received for college. Their comments seem to run parallel to Peggy's anger at what she sees as a "caste system" in which wealthier communities are able to offer their children a better education simply by virtue of their wealth and the value of their property. Although not directly cited in their talk, the issue of fairness in school funding has dominated public discourse in Michigan all fall and winter with the state legislature meeting almost nonstop to find a compromise way to handle its systemic inequalities.

An exchange ensues in which Peggy, citing Kozol, presses the issue of fairness while Misty and Nell try to explain why their schools are so well endowed. In debatelike fashion, the speakers offer assertions and refutations and seem fixed on winning. Misty and Nell argue for the fairness of a system in which affluent parents can enhance the opportunities of their children. Peggy counters that poorer parents actually pay taxes at as high or a higher rate but are able to raise less money for their children's education because the system is unfairly based on the value of the property or the wealth of a community.

**Misty:** Well, its just because everybody who lives there has the money to do it.

**Peggy:** And there's really a caste system.

**Nell:** It's the same thing in Bloomfield Hills and Pontiac. It's all property taxes that pay for it. And the property, you know, the property in Bloomfield Hills is worth a lot more.

**Peggy:** But that's not all and what I'm actually learning is this.

**Nell:** But, see, a lot of it is.

Additionally, Peggy sees a kind of systemic unfairness that extends beyond property tax and claims that other subsidies are extended to schools, particularly in middle- and upper class communities. She cites an example from Kozol's book:

**Peggy:** I mean, and they'll take, and one, a White, like high-rise complex moved in and was middle class. And they said they wanted a new school, so they built them a new school while the Black people stayed at the other school. Public. This is public. And it wasn't property tax. It was just; it was more than just property tax. They were being blatantly

**Misty:** A lot of what we have comes from parents, not necessarily from taxes, but

**Nell:** donations

**Misty:** through clubs.

**Peggy:** Through what?

**Nell:** Boosters.

**Misty:** Through clubs, like we have, we have the New Trier Club. And the New Trier Club is parents only, and its parents of the majority of athletes. And every year they have a New Trier Club brunch, which is strictly donations put toward the athletes and their equipment. And that's where most of our money comes from, it's from parents' donations and everything.

**Nell:** Bloomfield Hills is the same way.

During this period, several features mark the dialogue. First, the other participants remain quiet while Misty, Nell, and Peggy exhibit high degrees of joint involvement. In addition, Misty and Nell speak almost in chorus quickly completing one another's thoughts without appearing to interrupt. As the turn exchanges among Misty, Nell, and Peggy quicken, all the other participants remain silent. They do not even voice "backchannel" communication such as murmurs of assent or disagreement. I make a move to break the debatelike pattern, reframing the dialogue by inviting other speakers to contribute, linking this discussion to thinking about the differences between their own home communities and the places where they are student teaching as follows:

**Susan:** Do you like . . . (to Julie) I know you went to Oakwood [pseudonym].

**Julie:** Ummhmm.

**Susan:** You mentioned that last time we had dinner together. That's . . . there's a real difference between the school where you went as a student—some other people mentioned it, too—and the school where you work. Do you notice it in things like materials or . . .

**Julie:** Definitely.

This move to reframe briefly engenders a series of echoing personal narratives. Julie, Marcia, and Lia, the three participants who heretofore have not spoken, offer them. Each tells a brief anecdote illustrating the poverty of the schools in which they work. They deal with the lack of art teachers, gym teachers, and counselors. But, in each case, the speaker tells a resigned story of making due with insufficient resources. Peggy responds by reintroducing the issue of fairness that has only temporarily been put aside. Referring to a guidance counselor who has been described as having a caseload so heavy that he can spend less than 10 minutes with a child and frequently has to "bump" his appointments, she says:

**Peggy:** But how could you want to stay? Like, I feel for him, too, because how can he feel, I mean, its frustrating. I would rather not do the job than have to not do it well.

Misty, who has to this point been at odds with Peggy, adds what appears to be her assent, addressing Peggy directly and saying:

**Misty:** And it makes me so interested, Peggy, because the image you're getting is, like, I can see where it would make you so furious and it does make, like, that's the thing that's so hard for me is that we talk about this a lot, too.

With this remark, Misty expresses interest in the issue Peggy has framed as well as her attempt to see Peggy's point of view and the difficulty these conflicting views cause her.

**Misty:** And the thing that's so hard is, I totally don't think, like as an educator, I don't think its fair that there's that drastic a difference, but as a student and a person who grew up where I did, yeah, the competition is a little overwhelming, but the privileges, I would not trade them for the world.

**Nell:** See, I feel the same tug you're in.

Peggy replies, "I can understand that. And its not, and I don't mean it to sound like I'm attacking you or anything." But she continues to voice her anger. Nell restates Misty's compromises position—that it is possible to be angered about the unfairness as a teacher but grateful for the opportunities as a student.

**Nell:** See, I feel that, that same, that same anger, you know, especially when we sat there in my class my sophomore year and watched this thing that this big television station had done about our school and compared it to Pontiac. And, as a teacher, I go, "this is just so insane," you know, that five miles down the road they're canceling the football team. They're canceling all the sports because they can't afford to have them. And at my school they're making them up, you know.

Peggy interjects, "I grew up in a school like that." This personal revelation changes the thrust of her position. Until now, she has used Kozol's book and his analysis as the source of her claims to authoritative knowledge and challenged Nell and Misty to account for their schools and experience in personal terms. Now, however, she reveals that her school experience was as impoverished as that which Kozol describes. Additionally, she makes it clear that she does not share her peers' experience of conflict between their "student" and "teacher" perspectives on this issue.

In a sense, Peggy begins to become one with the textual example—a process of transparency or interpenetrating of text and talk, character and conversational role, identified by Wortham (1995) as a "participant example." Peggy's assertion makes it difficult for participants to find an easy consensus. It underscores strong differences among club members in values and identities forged in their early experiences of family and community. Here, differences among club members echo those that may be insidiously operant when, as some of the published autobiographers describe, diverse teachers and pupils meet each other on the presumed common ground of public education.

During these exchanges, it is again notable that the other club members remain silent. Peggy, Misty, and Nell continue to wrestle with the difficult issues of fairness and the gaps in their own experiences due to differences in wealth. Peggy describes the poverty of her school—the higher and higher millages levied to raise money for schools and the lack of a strong real estate base such that despite the millages, the community is forced to cancel services as basic as school buses and as important as advanced placement courses.

Nell and Misty counter with the quality of their academic preparation for college, again stressing their gratitude for the education they have received.

> **Nell:** And it was at that point, my first term, my freshman year in college, my dad saw my grades and went, "you sure this isn't too easy for you?" I was so prepared for college, and I look back on that and I'm thankful that I was able to go to a school like Goddard [pseudonym].

She and Misty think aloud about what would happen to that experience if some of the resources they enjoyed were shared with less affluent districts.

> **Misty:** At the same time, is it fair to let those other kids sit at the bottom.

> **Nell:** Let them sit at the bottom or should we all have the same thing because, really, there's not the money to bring them up here.

Their repetition of the phrase "let them sit at the bottom" heightens the sense of conflict by separating "us" and "them" and implying that wealthier districts need to decide the fate of poorer ones. This solution is also less than satisfactory because it incurs a cost to wealthy districts to "bring up" the educational experiences of poorer youngsters. They venture another possible solution that they see as avoiding the economic and power questions: better teaching. If teachers in poorer schools taught better, students might learn better there.

Nell asks, "What's so expensive about teaching someone to be prepared to write?" But Marcia, who is a good friend of Peggy's (and actually gave her Kozol's book as a Christmas gift) speaks after a long silence. She joins the argument to say, in support of Peggy's position, "Paying the teachers. Paying the teachers who will do that." Peggy follows her, and they form a coalition briefly voicing a response to the solution offered by Nell and Misty:

**Peggy:** No, but they don't want to. I'll tell you, because their school isn't even set up so that learning is important because it smells. They have leaks everywhere. They have, I mean, these schools, I mean

**Marcia:** They're unfit for

**Peggy:** Yeah, they were unfit to even, yeah, to be in. And when the environment was so, they're so dreary and desolate. I mean, how can you expect kids to want to learn? And when basically, and this is what the mayor of Chicago said, "Well we don't wanta, it would be like giving money to these schools would be like rearranging the deck chairs on the Titanic." And that's when I actually stopped reading because I thought I'm getting too emotional.

## DODGING HOT LAVA:
## REFRAMING AND REPAIR

I initiate a transitional period of reframing and repair following Peggy's statement that she was too emotional to continue reading Kozol's book. It is a period normalizing the conflict that emerged in Phase 1. In making this transition, the group begins to reorient its talk to Angelou's book. My attempt at reframing the discussion has a hostlike, social etiquette function. It is a move I attempted unsuccessfully earlier in the meeting when I intervened to try to get more speakers involved and broaden the debate's content so that others (who had not read *Savage Inequalities* or come from the community under scrutiny) might have a chance to speak. But far from being taken by the participants as directive (as might, for instance, be the case if I were the group's teacher), the first of my gambits was only briefly successful in quelling the conflict in which three of the members are going over the same ground without apparent resolution. As the conflict again ensued, the other three members (Julie, Lia, and Marcia) and I fell silent.

Only now, after substantially more heated talk does my effort at reframing apparently succeed. I initiate it by making reference to an anecdote in Angelou's text, which is related to the theme of the preceding debate. The text is one all members can discuss. It poses the problem under discussion in a less directly personal way, moving from debate about one member's affluent suburb and in contrast to another member's poor high school to a broader discussion of inequality and even the different expectations people hold for youngsters from more and less affluent backgrounds. Coincidentally, and unbeknownst to me, the vignette I cite is precisely the one the other members have already discussed in one of their courses and with which they began the evening:

> **Susan:** I was thinking, when I was listening to this, about a scene in the book of her graduation.
>
> **Nell:** Yeah, that's how this got started.
>
> **Susan:** Oh, did it? Because, you know, there you have the case where she was actually very academically able.
>
> **Others:** Unnhmm.
>
> **Susan:** She was reading Shakespeare in elementary school, or whatever, and there were students in her school who were learning a lot, but you saw when the guy from the school board made the talk
>
> **Nell:** The speech
>
> **Susan:** And said they're gonna get these materials and these labs or whatever and you guys are going to get new blacktop for your <u>basketball</u>
>
> **Nell:** <u>Basketball</u> courts
>
> **Susan:** That, what was crushing was the expectations that other people had for them.
>
> **Lia:** No hope.

**Misty:** Yeah, you can only do so well.

**Susan:** And I think about your schools that, where maybe the teaching was better. Maybe it wasn't. But you're dealing with a group of students who expect to excel and whom everybody else in the society expects to excel.

It is notable that Nell and I say the word, "basketball," simultaneously. Like the earlier topic-finding talk in which, referencing the film, *Boyz in the Hood*, the tracking of African-American students into athletics was critiqued, this part of Angelou's vignette taps a consensus that, perhaps because it is of no direct cost to the members, seems easy and welcome. Also, significantly, I reframe the problem that anchored the debate until now, not as economic injustice or racism, but as the "crushing expectations that other people had for them." This is a troubling move for several reasons.

Until this point, the three dominant speakers have debated a very important problem in public education in Michigan and elsewhere. Their comments, in fact, voiced most of the major viewpoints of the political constituencies debating the problem in the legislature and the press. Here, however, is an instance where the debate, although powerful and expressive of the entering positions of the speakers, is also troublesome. It threatens the continuation of conversation because the three speakers are approaching an apparent impasse and, like Peggy reading Kozol's book, may become "too emotional" to continue. Further threatening the conversation and the group is the fact that their talk has effectively marginalized the rest of the members and the book they have read in common.

In making a hostlike move away from conflict, however, I seem to sacrifice discussion of an important issue in order to restore cooperative participation in the group. My comment deflects the group's attention from Peggy's concern and misses an opportunity to help participants stand back from the solutions they are offering to see how they may be workable or limited. Also prevented by this move is a reflective examination of participants' entering positions and a chance to reconsider them in light of new information or at least see why and how they come into conflict with strongly held views of others. Ironically, the pressure to maintain conversation as a social (and sociable) event seems to run at odds with the group's exploring the relationship between students' primary socialization in the home and community and their experience of the public world of formal education. And, derailing talk as one participant grows "emotional," we back away from the related, and very uncomfortable, topic of race. The dilemma for a teacher in such a situation might be that of managing argument and examination of difference within the in the medium of conversation and without risking its breakdown.

With my reframing, however, participation proliferates in a kind of conversation repair effort, shoring up participants involvement and sociability. Virtually all members with the exception of Peggy offer examples of the effects of community expectations on their school experience. "Expectation" is a topic on which almost everyone appears able to weigh in without apparent risk of direct conflict. Much of the ensuing repair work concerns the damaging effects of adult expectations in both poor and affluent communities.

This segment is capped by a poignant narrative told by Nell in which a high school senior in her class commited suicide because he did not receive admission to a college of the stature expected by his parents and community. In this narrative, Nell returns the group to a consideration of the deeply personal consequences of being educated within communities. She hints at the danger of stereotyping more affluent students as immune to difficulty, balancing Peggy's (and Angelou's) descriptions of the difficulties students face in virtue of racism and economic hardship.

> **Nell:** You know, it's really. They took a lot of pressure off my class. There's a lot going on, like parental pressure and societal pressure in my town got really down on the schools about, you know, only 35% of the class last year went to U of M. "We should be sending 50%." They really got down on it. And all of a sudden the parental pressure was so strong that we had, and we had a guy in my chemistry class my junior year and I remember him talking about, "I just sent my application off to the University of Chicago or Chicago University

> **Misty:** University of Chicago.

> **Nell:** And he really wanted to get into the University of Chicago. His dad went to the University of Chicago. This was a big family thing. He got deferred. I saw him this whole year. Spring break I came back, and he wasn't there. And I said

> **Misty:** His dad pulled him out?

> **Nell:** And I said, what happened? And they said, I can't remember his name now, it was a foreign name, but they said, "Oh, didn't you hear?" And I said,

"What?" And they said, "Well, he got his rejection from Chicago and *killed himself.*" That it was that much pressure to go to Chicago.

As resolution binds all the group members as future teachers (and regardless of their social and economic backgrounds), a phase of synthesis begins in which they offer and build on one another's personal narratives. They talk about having violated community expectations by choosing to attend the state university and become elementary school teachers—a solution that "works" regardless of whether the community from which participants come is rich or poor.

Six of the seven participants speak during the period of repair and transition offering personal or book-related commentary. Thus, the group reasserts itself *as a group.* They move from a particularly personal and heated topic to Angelou's book and some consensus about the damaging effects of expectations that do not take individual talents and motives into account. Thus, they manage to sustain coherent and polite conversation in the face of threats to its continuation that developed in the topic-finding phase. In forging this consensus, however, Peggy retreats in silence, her critical comments about fairness pushed to the margins.

Ironically, it is the binding power of these reframing and repair narratives, that originally stood out as noteworthy in my fieldnotes, and initial analysis of this meeting. Yet, lacking at that time either a fuller account of the meeting conversation or insight into the conflict that preceded this phase of talk, the cooperative, narrative way of speaking evidenced here was over generalized and much of the meeting's complexity was missed. Not only was the struggle that preceded them overlooked, but the group's turning away from Peggy's concerns was also missed.

Reframing in avoidance of difficult topics or disagreement is a discourse move that appeared in numerous book club conversations among both the preservice and experienced teachers with whom I worked in the book clubs. A related analysis of our experienced teacher participants discussing the books of Angelou in the Literary Circle by Glazier et al., 2000, for example, found that participants tended to veer discursively away from difficult topics. Among these difficult topics was race, and we can see in the example cited here that I was instrumental in trying to move the conversation back from this topic.

Using the metaphor of "hot lava" from the playground game in which children attempt to run as fast a possible from one point to another without dipping their feet into the imaginary substance, Glazier argued that book club conversations could be relatively smoothly orchestrated to do the same. However, that avoidance of conflict and difficulty had the effect of shortening speakers' engagement with a topic. Hot lava topics proliferated in our book club discussions of Angelou's work. Glazier observes that

> Angelou's use of poetics—her use of humor, irony, and exaggeration, for example—can leave a White reader unsure how to respond to the injustices that Angelou confronts in her life and then writes about in her texts. When these readers arrive at topics raised within the texts, they were unsure how to engage them. To do so meant learning an alternative "discourse" (Gee, 1989) or way of speaking and thinking about oneself and others. Over time in sustained, collaborative contexts (the book club and Literary Circle) and through the use of alternative texts (autobiographies), participants inched toward these challenging issues. Teachers began to move through these silenced topics into unsettling, but imperative, discourse. (P. 296)

With time, trust, and experience, Glazier found that speakers entertain hot lava topics for longer periods of time and in greater detail. But a major challenge to teaching and learning by means of conversation is introducing and sustaining hot lava topics on the conversational floor—and examining them in ways that do not veer from conflict yet maintain the conversation as a speech event.

## BELIEVING: JOINT INQUIRY

The repair work of participants initiated as we backed away from the hot lava of talk about race and inequality was a decidedly mixed blessing. As mentioned earlier, it occasions the avoidance of a very important theme by the group. Yet the reframing and repair work undertaken also marks a shift in conversational genre from doubting/debating to "believing" and the telling of coordinating rather than competing narratives in order to advance understanding. In the joint inquiry phase of the conversation, we see few examples of the prior pattern of assertion and refutation that dominated the debate phase. Moreover, we see an increase in the telling of personal vignettes and a shift in the function of these vignettes from pressing a moral point in contradiction to one asserted by another speaker's turn to the accumulation of stories whose accumulated moral points cluster around a single question or idea.

Joint inquiry offers multiple examples of the "believing game" played in pursuit of questions about meaning. It is occasionally punctuated by "doubting," which serves to push the believers farther along in their efforts at sense-making, but this doubting is of the accumulating consensus rather than of the claims made by a particular speaker. It begins by Peggy speaking at the end of the transition. Rising again to lead by introducing or recycling a topic, Peggy's comments are now more encompassing of the group and Angelou's book. She does not relinquish her earlier interest in equality, but reframes it in terms of Angelou's experiences and writing:

> **Peggy:** I guess my big question was, that I actually asked . . . there were so many things you could be angry about in here, and it was amazing, but how did she rise above this. And the question I had asked, so, *why does the caged bird sing*? Like why does she remain, I'm thinking that means that a caged bird
>
> **Misty:** Shining through, so to speak.
>
> **Peggy:** Like she hangs in there and still, yeah. She keeps trudging along, kind of, thinking, why does a caged bird sing? With all this oppression and discrimination and unfairness and unjustness in the world, she keeps going. And she keeps struggling. *But why*?

In asking her question, Peggy restates her anger and directs her interrogation to the book rather than to Misty and Nell. Misty interjects, but this time to contribute to the framing of Peggy's question, and other members speak to shed light on the difficult question posed by Peggy. These responses are offered in an additive way as the group begins to form a tentative working consensus. However, in a kind of conceptual "scaffolding," at intervals the group's comfort with this consensus is disturbed by a doubting speaker (alternately Julie, Lia, Peggy, and myself) who "ups the conceptual ante," urging the group to work harder to solve the textual problem Peggy has posed. Julie wonders, for example, if the book is really representative of the experience of a broad range of African Americans. I suggest that Maya's "singing" was sustained by her family. As this possible explanation gains momentum, Lia questions it, remarking that she found Maya's grandmother to be cold and her parents inattentive.

This leads to an extended sequence in which different participants offer brief vignettes to extend or elaborate on the idea that family support can sustain a person through difficult times and that the ways families express that support might differ as a function of cultural style. Marked in this section are both the coordinating (rather than conflicting) quality of the narratives participants tell and also their more abbreviated quality, serving less as full-blown expositions of a speaker's point of view than as an extension of other's speakers stories. This appears to win Lia over to the accumulating consensus. She speaks of Momma as follows:

> **Lia:** Like, I see, you could tell she loved her. The grandmother loved her but it's just the way she showed it. Through the hardness and the, it's just different.

> **Nell:** Kind of military sergeant-type thing. In that they may be hard on you and they may always be driving you and pushing you, but you know that they care about you but they just don't

> **Julie:** She knows it, too. I mean if you saw the interview [that Angelou gave on television prior to her delivering her inaugural poem].

> **Misty:** Yeah.

> **Julie:** <u>She</u>

> **Misty:** <u>She</u> knew.

> **Julie:** The way she talks about her grandmother, you know that she just respected the heck out of her.

> **Marcia:** Well, so many people aren't comfortable with acting that way. You know, I know from my personal experience that my parents are, my mother is kind of domineering and my parents don't feel comfortable showing, like saying I love you, and its not a huggy, touchy family

> **Misty:** We don't say it in my house either.

> **Marcia:** But I've never doubted for an instant that they didn't . . . I mean they showed it in different ways. I mean my parents showed it through sacrificing for us and always doing whatever they could for us. And I think that's kind of how the grandmother showed it through a different <u>way.</u>

> **Misty:** *A* <u>different</u> way.

> **Nell:** Yeah.

**Lia:** She did. [Like the example when they were] coming from the dentist.

**Marcia:** Yeah.

This sequence continues with more personal accounts of club members' parents and grandparents who appear to have difficulty expressing words of love but who, apparently like Maya's grandmother, show love in their actions. This sequence is marked not only by brief, coordinating personal narratives, but also by the interweaving of references to Maya's life (available both in her book and in her televised recent interview). It also contrasts notably with the debate phase in the number of participants speaking, the repetition of one another's words and phrases, and in participants speaking before others' turns are completed without negative sanction. In short, this period appears highly involved and collaborative.

However, Peggy, who posed the initial question about Maya's persistence in the face of difficulty, does not add to the accumulating consensus. She sits quietly, listening attentively and looking at each speaker. Several more personal narratives illustrate the power of Momma's love to support Maya. Then Peggy restates her question in a form of assessment akin to teachers who, having initiated a question and heard out a number of student replies convey to the group that the answers have not sufficed by their restatement of the question.

**Peggy:** Well, I just don't think that's enough of an explanation. I don't, I mean I think its part of one, but I don't, its not enough for me yet, to believe that that's why she kept going. There's got to be something else to me. I believe family is enough but . . .

Peggy hedges her criticism with her introductory "well" and her acknowledgment that what the group is saying is "part of" an explanation. She also lets her voice (and turn) trail off, as if inviting further talk. This is not a throwing down of the gauntlet or a challenge to any individual. It is a move to provoke the group to think harder and further. It carries particular power since it is offered by Peggy, who began this round of problem solving with the question, "So why *does* the caged bird sing?"

This doubting of the emerging consensus by various speakers is an interesting dialogic move in the club's social context because it demonstrates how conversation can serve to encourage speakers' thinking about the book in ways they might not have ventured alone. The teacher typically undertakes this kind of move in classrooms. In the book club conversation, it is not the host/organizer alone, but various members who push the group to think harder. Thus members have an opportunity to assert influence in framing and reframing the group's joint pursuit of meaning. The conversational work undertaken in response to this scaffolding weaves together personal response to the book (often in the form of individual vignettes) with careful reference to the author's language and imagery. Both readers' personal experiences and the text's elements are used as sources on which to base interpretations.

We can see this move as "scaffolding" of participants' thought in the sense that it fosters exploration of the book and its themes beyond what individual participants might undertake if they were to read and think about the book alone without benefit of conversation. "Scaffolding" is by now a well-known (and perhaps well worn) metaphor coined by Bruner (1974) initially accounting for the dynamic nature of infants' language learning in dialogue with their mothers. Of this process, Bruner said, "mothers most often see their role as supporting the child in achieving an intended outcome, entering only to assist, reciprocate, or "scaffold" the interaction" (p. 12). This idea of assisted performance is strongly resonant with Vygotsky's (1978) theories of cognitive development and has been the source of much interest and investigation in contemporary psychological and educational research.

Psychologists have argued that learning occurs in a zone of proximal development (Newman, Griffin, & Cole, 1989). Learning in that zone involves activity just beyond what the individual learner is capable of accomplishing by her or himself, and that the effect of dialogue on learning in the zone is that the learner is able to do, initially with assistance, what he or she cannot yet do alone. Gradually, with internalization, the learner achieves independence and is able to perform unassisted—that is, of course, until he or she encounters a new and difficult challenge. In dialogue among peers, performance can also be assisted, both by the ways dialogue exposes multiple ways of framing and answering questions and by the way it "collects" or accumulates the different background knowledge of participants. What is interesting to discover in peer conversation is its potential to recycle questions thereby pushing discussion further and challenging participants to reason through difficult quests or problems. Of this experience, Julie commented in her sketchbook, "Its amazing how some connections aren't made until you hear someone else talking about it" (Sketchbook, 2/4/93).

Peggy pressed the group gently to move on with their effort to answer her question, and this took the group back into Angelou's narrative as follows:

**Peggy:** Yeah, well, I think that's important (i.e., family love), but I'm saying, I guess I'd be interested to hear what else...I mean what was her driving force?

**Marcia:** Well, I think a big part of what I read, in just little bits and piece throughout the book, is that she felt, to me, I was that she was a woman who knew she was capable of a lot. I felt like she was aware of how brilliant she was. And I felt that she knew that she could really do something. You know, maybe I'm reading into it, but I felt she had a real sense of

**Susan:** She had a gift . . .

**Marcia:** One, I'm really brilliant, and two, I can really make it out and do something really special and make a difference.

Interestingly, however, family love remains on the table as a source of explanation. Lia interjects, for example at this point, "Bailey [Maya's brother] kept her going." What is impressive about the next sequence of scaffolded conversation is the group's effort to coordinate these two possible explanations and not force an either/or conclusion. An extended sequence of reporting examples from the book in which both family and nonfamily people close to Maya contributed to her learning that she had talent and possibilities beyond the crushing defeat implied in the graduation speech.

This sequence culminates with the group lingering on a passage from the book in which Maya describes an encounter with her mother that occurs, in fact, at age 20—actually past the end of this book's narrative. Maya recounts a visit to her mother's house in San Francisco after her own son had been born. She describes declining her mother's offer of a ride in preference to the street car—itself a rich image of Maya's earlier efforts to assert her independence and power by becoming the first and only female streetcar conductor in San Francisco. She writes, "And we were at the very bottom of the hill and she knew I wouldn't take a ride from her, that I would take the streetcar. That I had to own myself. And she said, "You know, Baby, I think you are the greatest woman I ever met." Yet even this moment of revelation leaves the group only momentarily satisfied, and the cycle of scaffolded conversation continues:

**Misty:** There's also . . .

**Peggy:** That's amazing. What does she mean by "being part of the earth?"

**Marcia:** Part of it? I think actually feeling she belonged.

**Misty:** I kind of think the opposite, like she's special. Like instead of just part of everybody, she also stands above it. She's different, kind of, and just, I just see her rising up.

These sequences illustrate a merging of personal, autobiographical response to text with a close reading of the author's work that college teachers of literacy are now arguing is the essence of authentic response. According to Beach (1993), we currently know little about the role that teachers' implicit theories of response play in the way they shape literacy discussion in their own classrooms. Exchanges like these bring together two kinds of responses available in the future teachers' repertoire and recombine them in ways that enable them to do something that research on teacher and college student discussion finds difficult. In these responses, readers entertain multiple, sometimes competing explanations or hypotheses and sustain intellectual effort through difficult material in order to build theories or test explanations (Torres-Peterson & John-Steiner, 1995). Thus, in joint inquiry we have an activity in which, by merging believing and doubting, participants are able to achieve, however briefly, rigorous intellectual examination of a book and an idea while sustaining a sense of "connected knowing" (Belenky et al., 1986) that does not put conversational involvement at risk.

A close look at our talk discloses the considerable work participants undertake to manage interaction. We cannot envision a zone of learning in which talk is transparent. The "how" of our interactions in this zone is intimately woven with the "what" of our talk. What we can learn with peers and/or more experienced others (be they teachers who may be present at the table or authors who are present in their texts) is rooted in and related to our conversations. Implicit in the idea of such conversations is the development of a community within which learning from text can occur. The next chapter illustrates, with examples from the 2-year book club of experienced teachers called The Literary Circle, how sustained conversation over multiple texts brings participants closer to one another, to an exploration of the idea of culture, and to the hot lava topic of racism.

# CHAPTER 9

# Culture Across Texts and Contexts: The Literary Circle

As seen throughout this book, culture is a conceptual moving target. Complex and powerful, it is an idea whose definition is contested and whose boundaries are mapped with difficulty. As a lived and living process of meaning and making meaning in contact with others, we all participate in learning and creating culture. The challenge for teacher education, then, is not only to acknowledge one's own background and the backgrounds of others, although these are clearly important, but to wonder—to inquire critically into those backgrounds as they have helped shape, texture, and bias the ways we live our lives as teachers and learners. This is difficult work. Far from faking being Polish, this aspect of professionalism involves discovering one's own life story—or that of another—by risking uncertainty about meaning and being open to possibility.

Literature educator Reed Dasenbrock (1992) describes this process as one of education to "develop curiosity about" rather than "expert knowledge of" culture. What we need, he says, is a way of telling, hearing and reading stories of self not to "possess" their meanings or demonstrate "knowledge already in place . . . but as a scene of learning "(p. 39). For many teachers, both beginning and experienced, this way of thinking about learning is unfamiliar. It requires a literature and a way of teaching about culture stressing not rationalization and generalization, but uncertainty, imagery, dialogue, and story.

## THE LITERARY CIRCLE

Contemporary anthropologists remind us that cultural experience is accessible by recollection as well as by observation and description, by looking within as well as without. Looking inward, of course, can be taken to extremes. Ethnography is not autobiography, although ethnography depends on much self-reflection. And Euro-American teachers should be cautious not to use self-examination as a way, once again, to avoid looking at cultural complexities—especially racism. Yet it is almost impossible to understand racial, linguistic, and economic inequality without looking at one's own autobiography—how one's consciousness is formed in and through our interactions with others.

My teaching and research over the past several years has been about investigating ways we might employ conversation and personal narrative to challenge and support Euro-American teachers to look both outward and inward as they educate an increasingly diverse pupil population. In this book, I have so far described one context for this work: an informal undergraduate Future Teachers' Autobiography Club. But I also designed and taught a course for experienced teachers called, "Culture, Literacy and Autobiography," and took part in and researched the course members' subsequent voluntary book club, The Literary Circle. This research was undertaken with my colleague, Taffy Raphael, as well as our research assistants Mary McVee, Susan Wallace-Cowell, Jocelyn Glazier, and Bette Shellhorn. Our project combined two lines of work. The first was my work, with Julie deTar, described in the preceding chapters. That work focused on the learning of beginning teachers' learning about culture. The second, led by Taffy Raphael, focused on reading, writing, and talking about literature in peer-led book clubs to foster youngsters' comprehension and critical thinking.

The teacher participants in the autobiography course and the Literary Circle were all experienced. They were returning to the university to study for their master's degrees in literacy instruction. Like the student teachers described earlier in this book, these teachers were Euro-American, female, monolingual speakers of English, and from lower and middle-income backgrounds. Some registered for the autobiography course because they were interested in exploring culture. Others were drawn to the idea of reading and discussing literature with other teachers. A few took the course simply because it fulfilled an elective slot in their program and met on an evening that conveniently fit their busy schedules.

All of the students remained together for the duration of the course, "Culture, Literacy and Autobiography," and then for a voluntary monthly book club, the Literary Circle. Including summers, we met for 2 years, held 26 book clubs, and read as many books. I selected for our first 6 book clubs the autobiographies I had previously read with the Future Teachers' Autobiography Club. I was eager to read and discuss them again, this time within a classroom-based book club format and with more experienced teachers. After the course ended, the class decided by consensus to read either the second book by each author (whether or not these were autobiographies) or another book in that author's body of work. The remaining 12 books were suggested by teachers in the Literary Circle and chosen on the basis of group deliberations.

I studied the course and club with my colleagues. In a design similar to that with which Julie deTar and I researched the Future Teachers' Autobiography Club, we collected data, both written and oral, documenting the teachers' experience. As I taught the course, Taffy Raphael joined as a participant-observer. Three graduate students also served as participant-observers. The students were aware of the study and gave consent to participate. During the course, I was unaware of each student's decision about participating and did not analyze class work as part of the research until the course ended. Near the end of the course, I asked the class members if they would like to continue to meet and talk about culture and autobiographies. They enthusiastically responded, and our voluntary book club began. At that point, an additional research assistant joined the group, and we moved toward a collaborative research design in which teachers as well as university-based participants shared openly in the process of inquiring into our learning.

We documented the activities that took place the master's course and subsequent club in five ways:

1. During the course, I maintained an *instructor's journal* detailing both weekly observations of the class and ongoing questions, concerns, and instructional decisions.

2. The other researchers engaged as participant observers in the course and the Literary Circle, writing *fieldnotes* immediately after each meeting.

3. All book discussions were *audiotaped* while two were also videotaped for analysis.

4.  *Written texts* produced by the teachers were collected and studied.
5.  All teachers were *interviewed* about the book club experience.

Our research was premised on the idea that learning begins and ends on the social plane (Gavelek & Raphael, 1996). As a function of oral and written engagement with others (and with written text), we hypothesized that teachers would experience transformations in their thinking about culture, literacy, and autobiography. We further hypothesized that they would express those transformations in subsequent cycles of communicative activity. Data collection and analysis, therefore, focused on the social and linguistic "traces" of teacher learning. We, therefore, used techniques drawn from ethnography and sociolinguistics, including the following:

1.  The gradual refinement of research questions and the inductive development of analytic categories grounded in continuous comparison of data as they were collected.
2.  Triangulation among different kinds and sources of data to cross-check inferences about participants' understandings.
3.  Collaborative analysis of conversations, interviews, and written texts for insights into the ways participants represented their ideas and negotiated them in social interaction with others.

Approaching this work with a social historical lens, we developed case studies highlighting changes in participants' ways of communicating with one another about the autobiographies, their own literate and cultural backgrounds, and their work as teachers (Florio-Ruane et al., 1997; Glazier et al., 2000). Our research took four forms: conversational analysis of our talk over time in book clubs; analysis of the forms and functions of personal stories told by participants in those conversations as part of their response to the autobiographies; tracking of intertextual references, or the ways our conversations references books and their themes over time; and descriptions of participants' extensions of what they were doing in the book clubs to other areas of their professional lives.

## THINKING TOGETHER

Figure 9.1 lists the books read in the course and in the subsequent Literary Circle. Because the teachers participated in the selection of 75% of the texts we read, analysis of the text set and the teachers' selection and refer-

**FIG. 9.1**  *Books Read in the Course and in the Literary Circle*

**Books Read in Course (September–December, 1995)**
Vivian Paley, *White Teacher*
Maya Angelou, *I Know Why the Caged Bird Sings*
Eva Hoffman, *Lost in Translation*
Richard Rodriguez, *Hunger of Memory*
Jill Ker Conway, *The Road from Coorain*
Mike Rose, *Lives on the Boundary*

**Books Read in Literary Circle (January–August, 1996)**
Vivian Paley, *Kwanzaa and Me*
Maya Angelou, *Gather Together in My Name*
Eva Hoffman, *Exit Into History*
Richard Rodriguez, *Days of Obligation: An Argument with My Mexican Father*
Jill Ker Conway, *True North*
Mike Rose, *Possible Lives*
Eudora Welty, *One Writer's Beginnings*
Zora Neal Hurston, *Their Eyes Were Watching God*

**Books Read in Literary Circle (September 1996–August 1997)**
Peggy Ornstein, *Schoolgirls*
Jung Chang, *Wild Swans*
Amy Tan, *The Kitchen God's Wife*
Toni Morrison, *Song of Solomon*
Kim Chernin, *In My Mother's House*
Mary Catherine Bateson, *Composing a Life*
James McBride, *The Color of Water*
Esmeralda Santiago, *When I Was Puerto Rican*
Frank McCourt, *Angela's Ashes*
Mary Crow Dog, *Lakota Woman*
Alice Walker, *In Search of Our Mother's Gardens*
Victor Villasenor, *Rain of Gold*

Full citations appear in References

encing of texts is of particular interest. As noted in the description of the Future Teachers' Autobiography Club, to select the initial text set of six autobiographies, I used a very simple scheme for book selection: I chose books to represent three categories: Euro-American teachers who reflected on their own cultural experiences as they taught students different from themselves; and authors roughly approximating Ogbu's (1987) categories of "voluntary" and "involuntary" immigrants. My purposes were twofold: to spark self-reflection and to illustrate that not all immigrant experiences are the same. However, by the second semester, when our class became a voluntary club, my typology was rapidly breaking down, and our understanding of culture growing more complex and multifaceted. As we read a second book by each author, we were plunged into conversations in which culture had no easy meaning. Its province was no longer that of immigrants or members of linguistic and racial minorities. One book by a member of an ethnic group was likely to lead to stereotyping, and so we read multiple books by members of particular ethnic groups. We read over historical period and genre.

By the second year of the club's existence the circle of our choices had widened to include autobiography, fiction, and even social research related to autobiography and identity. Moreover, we attended films and lectures related to the themes of our reading, including on-campus lectures by some of the authors we read, videotapes of television interviews with others, and films of some of the books as well as related subjects. This opportunity for extended reading and discussion across many texts was atypical of the professional development experiences usually available for learning either about culture of about literacy. Our participation in the monthly meetings immersed us in the kind of experiences Dewey (1938) might have called "educative"—firmly rooted in the present of our monthly meetings, reaching back into the past of our own and the published authors' remembered experiences, and leading us into a future of new texts to be discovered and new ways of understanding ourselves as teachers and as participants in the wider society.

The Literary Circle's duration as well as the emergent nature of its talk and texts pushed us beyond a model of "culture as ethnicity." As we did this, we began to identify within-group variation, similarities across the experiences of people from different ethnic groups; the power of other features of experience also to shape identity; and our own participation in culture, power, learning, and change. This kind of educative experience is not the stuff of a day-long workshop or even of a summer institute. But it is an example of sustainable teacher development—sustainable, literally, in the 2-year commitment its members made, and sustainable in the longer term impact that members have had both in their classrooms and in roles of leadership in a network of similar study groups (Clark, 2001). And, although the changing lives of its members meant that the group did not continue to meet in the same form after its second year, the Literacy Circle spawned a network of related groups across our state. In these networked study groups, both original members and newcomers continue to read together, study culture, write about their experiences, and attempt to bring the fruits of this experience into their work with youngsters in their classrooms (The Book Club *Plus* Group, 1999; Florio-Ruane & Raphael, 2001).

## READING CULTURE
## IN AUTOBIOGRAPHY: AXES OF MEANING

In the Literary Circle, we changed our minds about culture and also about reading. The book club was a living laboratory in which to investigate what it means to comprehend text, what is "generic" about the texts within a genre, and how we might think intertextually. Writing about immigrant literature, critic Sau-Ling Wong (1991) advises against rigidly imposing a generic text structure on authors' life stories. Regardless of whether this structure is applied across all autobiographies (i.e., "ethnic autobiography" as the generic) or to particular national or ethnic groups (i.e., "Italian American autobiographies"), much is missed in reading texts this way. Instead, she urges reading texts along multiple axes of meaning, and I found her suggestion helpful in beginning to capture how we chose what to read in the Literary Circle as well as how we talked about what we read—both the texts themselves and those texts in relation to others.

In Wong's terms, "different salient features are revealed when an autobiography is read with different intertexts." Thus, reading along different "provisional axes of organization" reveals a "speaking subject inscribed by multiple discourses, positioned in multiple subjectivities and situated in multiple historical contexts" (p. 160). Taken together, analyses of the conversationally embedded oral personal narratives as well as talk about the published text reveals that our readings of culture grew considerably richer, more varied, engaging, and provocative. By the time we had read all 26 texts, both genre boundaries and aspects of culture were becoming increasingly blurred. Within these discussions, we examined the following aspects of culture:

- Culture is dynamic, changing over time and with contact with other people, places and activities.
- Culture colors and is colored by the experience of attending school and becoming literate in that context.
- Culture is expressed differently by individuals and families, even among those of the same ethnic group.
- Culture exists even in the experience of "White teachers".
- Culture is appropriated, resisted, and changed by individuals.
- Culture is cross-cut in our society by other factors in the experience of individuals and families (e.g., age, gender, race, socioeconomic standing).

Notably, the extended reading list and period of time to discuss our responses permitted development of trust and rapport among members, opportunities to read more widely (i.e., across the experiences of authors from different ethnic groups) and deeply (i.e., reading more than one book by a person from a particular ethnic, racial, or linguistic background). And, by staying together for an extended period in a self-directed activity, we had a chance to create for and among ourselves a discourse community in which a great deal of meaning was shared and available for cross-referencing as we proceeded.

Following the "intertextual metaphor," prevalent reading research, participants were able sensibly to, in Hartman's (1991) terms, "transpose texts into other texts, absorb one text into another, and build a mosaic of intersecting texts" (p. 617). Like the criss-cross landscape that Spiro and his colleagues (1993/1997) argue is necessary to learning of complex concepts and practices, the books became a conceptual network or roadmap by which we could repeatedly traverse the cultural landscape.

Our research examined participants' views of their own learning and professional growth, drawing primarily on Wallace-Cowell's analysis of interview data and personal writing done by the teachers as part of course and club participation. The teachers reported learning about aspects of identity including (a) professional practice, (b) personal intellectual growth, and (c) participation in literacy as culturally grounded practice (Wallace-Cowell, cited in Glazier et al., 2000). Although we had hypothesized that they would learn about literacy and culture, a key *unanticipated* finding was that teachers reported discovering themselves as "thinkers" as a byproduct of their involvement in book discussions. Finding this prompted us to consider the general potential of peer-led, conversation in the professional development of teachers.

Repeatedly, teachers talked of the impact that participation had on their sense of professional agency. Specific references were made to creating book club groups in their school setting with other teachers in their building; having the confidence to present their curriculum work locally to colleagues within their school or district, as well as at state and national conferences; and continuing to enhance in their own intellectual lives as they met within the Literary Circle to confront those hot lava topics that they had for so long tended to avoid. Analyzing the teachers' writing and interviews for insight into this sense of agency, we identified several clear themes: (a) increased confidence in and expression of their ideas; (b) a new tendency to envision alternative "possible selves" as they thought about their futures as teachers and as citizens; (c) increased desire to pursue learning; and (d) a renewed passion for literature and its ideas. The opportunity to read challenging literature, talk about it with colleagues, and craft (and hear) one another's personal narratives enhanced teachers' sense of themselves not only as teachers, but as thoughtful participants in society.

Another striking outcome of participating in the book club was teachers' experience of coming to see themselves as cultural beings. As White, middle-class, monolingual females, few in the group initially thought they had any culture to speak of. Although not all expressed this directly (although a few actually stated that they "had no culture"), most saw themselves initially as being the "same." Asked, for example, in the initial course to develop vignettes dealing with their own socialization into culture, most drew a blank. Reading the work of authors such as Maya Angelou and Richard Rodriguez further intimidated them. Only over time did differences among themselves emerge that became the source of the discovery that they, indeed, participated in a range of diverse—and very interesting—cultural settings. Some differences were subtle, such as the differences between daughters of farmers and daughters of cattle ranchers (both represented in our group). Others were more distinct, such as growing up Catholic in contrast to growing up Jewish. One teacher, Hannah, for example, described her emerging insights into the diversity underlying her initial sense of group homogeneity stating, "We might all look very, very similar and very homogeneous, but *boy* do we come from different places" (Interview, July 1996).

As these differences were elaborated within both the published autobiographies and stories of our own experience, it became easier and more interesting for participants to craft their own "literacy narratives." In these stories, the teller captures aspects of coming of age within a particular community, tradition, and family by describing the kinds of texts and literacy events encountered or created there. Another teacher, Kate, developed a project for herself (extended ultimately to her development of a curriculum project for youngsters) in which she culled "artifacts" of her own coming of age as a woman, a Catholic, and the daughter of farmers. She brought to this documentary work a close analysis of personal books, photographs, and writings (Fieldnotes, December 1995). An important part of teacher learning in this project, then, was the gradual construal of "literacy" as more than learning skills and strategies. Literacy came to be understood as a cultural practice, and become literate as deeply entwined with the development of social identity.

## TOWARD DIALOGIC, LITERATURE-BASED TEACHER DEVELOPMENT

If we accept a model of learning occurring in our engagement with others (alternately peers and more experienced others), we can look for evidence in our study of learning not only on the part of teachers, but also among the project's teacher educator/researchers. We found increased leadership among the teachers over time and a shift in teacher educator/researchers' participation from project leader/initiators, to fellow club members. This shift was, in part, a function of our study's design, which featured the gradual release of control from university-based participants as teachers became more experienced reading and discussing ethnic autobiographical literature within the book club format. But to realize this "design" required, in fact, learning on all sides and ongoing negotiation among all participants of "who we are and what we are doing." The gradual transfer of control thus occasioned new and more complex learning on the part of both teachers and the university-based initiators of the project.

As the circle of leadership widened, changes occurred in decision making about what to read, why to read, and how to read. The multiple voices within the group discursively crafted an emergent, open-ended "syllabus" reaching far beyond the one with which the course had begun. It took the form of an expanding network of linked texts (both oral and written) that were read differently (primarily by citing and referring to texts in different ways over time—moving from the explicitly personal or critical/descriptive to a hybrid of these two ways of reading). Although the course provided a conceptual scaffold for this process, the collaboration among teachers, teacher educators, and researchers produced new activity setting. To highlight the jointly constructed nature of this process, I use the pronoun "we" to refer to the learning of researcher/teacher educators as well as classroom teachers. We identified the following five domains of learning-oriented change occasioned by our collaboration:

1. Defining the book club situation.
2. Shaping the thematic content of book club talk and text.
3. Defining culture in more complex ways.
4. Transforming ways of talking and ways of reading.
5. Reaching out to professional communities.

Teachers assumed increasing control of literature discussion as the course became a voluntary club. This involved relocation of the group first from a classroom at the university to the course instructor's home, and, finally, to a local bookstore and café, a neutral site selected by the teachers that continues to be the meeting place of the Literary Circle. It also involved naming the group, and collectively making decisions about when to add new members. Individuals were free to decide when to leave the group or when to miss a meeting. Related to this freedom was teacher participation in negotiating and planning meeting times in an ongoing way, in contrast to obligatory meeting times pre-set by the instructor and university calendar.

Taking an equal, even proprietary voice, the teachers determined the thematic content of much of book club conversation. This included selecting books and conversational topics, and planning the group's agenda. Here, we gradually opened the selection process from initial assigned books to the second semester's suggested books to the second year's group negotiation of books. Related to this negotiation came changes in genre (e.g., we included nonautobiographical, nonfiction books as well as autobiographical fiction in the second year) and content (e.g., we stressed gender more in Year 2 than we did in Year 1).

In Year 2, we included autobiographical novels (e.g., *The Kitchen God's Wife* by Amy Tan; *Their Eyes Were Watching God*, by Zora Neale Hurston), more autobiographies by and about female intellectuals and writers (e.g., *Composing a Life*, by Mary Catherine Bateson; *One Writer's Beginnings*, by Eudora Welty; Peggy Orenstein's case studies of young women's self-esteem in *Schoolgirls*); and books by more than one person from a nation or ethnic group (e.g., China: *Wild Swans*, by Jung Chang and Tan's *Kitchen God's Wife*; African Americans: Maya Angelou's *I Know Why the Caged Bird Sings* and *Gather Together in My Name*; Hurston's, *Their Eyes Were Watching God*; Toni Morrison's, *Song of Solomon,* and Alice Walker's *In Search of our Mothers' Gardens*). We also read books across gender, comparing the voices and experiences of men and women who criss-crossed borders of immigrant life in contemporary times (e.g., Frank McCourt's, *Angela's Ashes*; Esmeralda Santiago's, *When I was Puerto Rican*; Victor Villasenor's, *Rain of Gold*; James McBride's, *The Color of Water*; and Mary Crow Dog's *Lakota Woman*).

Changes in what we read led us to widen the lens in the club's consideration of diversity. It enriched and complicated our investigation of "culture" to include race, class, and gender, but also national and international history and politics, family structure, intellectual life, and religion. In many of the autobiographies, these elements of culture were nested in accounts of family history and intergenerational transformation. As such, the literature provided opportunities to compare and contrast people's experiences in different historical periods, societies, gender roles, and social strata—as well as across intercultural contact and transformation (e.g., Eva Hoffman's, *Exit into History*; Richard Rodriguez's, *Days of Obligation*; Eva Hoffman's, *Lost in Translation*; James McBride's, *The Color of Water*; Mike Rose's, *Possible Lives*; and Esmeralda Santiago's, *When I Was Puerto Rican*). Gradually, then, the group engaged in a more dynamic view of culture as a process lived by people in contact and in time, rather than a static set of characteristics of an individual or isolated group. And, to be sure, the idea of an autobiography being reducible merely to an "ethnic" one—the story of a "them" different from an "us" merely on the basis of nationality, mother tongue, or hue of skin, grew less and less appropriate.

## CHANGING TALK ABOUT TEXT

The changes described here were negotiated in the microprocesses of our conversational responses to text. As participants moved away from the course's more formal book club structure to a looser conversational response, we no longer had an instructor or formal assessment. Conversational leadership grew more informally negotiated from session to session and across periods of conversation within sessions. Hot lava topics became more common. In contrast to our early meetings, we now referred to them by this name and acknowledged their presence and difficulty. Participants engaged more readily in issues of class and race through the somewhat less forbidding (for this group) doors of gender, cross-cultural comparison, and history. Participants found that they could uncover and discuss sexism more readily than they could uncover racism. Yet books like *Their Eyes Were Watching God*, *Wild Swans*, and *The Kitchen God's Wife*, forced us to look at these issues in tandem. Similarly, it appeared easier for us to examine the historical, social, and political dimensions of oppression in distant societies and cultures than in our own.

Much like the student teachers in the Future Teachers' Autobiography Club, our earliest conversations accentuated the connections across our experiences, even at the expense of exploration of difference or conflict. Mentioned earlier in this book. McVee (1999) analyzed our discussion of *The Road from Coorain*, for example, and found a high degree of repetition in our dialogue and a press toward consensus. In the following example from her analysis of an early book club during the master's course, we can see two participants exchange turns smoothly, each linking her turn topically with what has been previously said thus weaving a sense of shared understanding and interpersonal connection. Each has grown up in a farming context, and each sees that experience to be connected to her understanding of Conway's autobiography. Here they are talking about the farmer's consciousness of weather:

Kate: Well, I know just the, what the nature and the weather thing

Hannah: Yeah, that affected me because being on a farm, where your dad is able to do and his farm hands in the course of the day has to do with the weather. You know and what you're gonna be able to accomplish in that day and, you know, it's all around the weather. The connection between nature . . .

Kate: I find myself even now, you know, like being very conscious of how many sunny days we've had in a row,

Hannah: Me too.

Kate: And how many rainy days we've had in a row.

Hannah: How are the farmers doing?

Note the high degree of involvement in the speakers' talk—completing one another's sentences, asserting agreement, repeating one another's key words or themes. One way to view this example is that participants are forming a kind of connected knowing in which they are responding to Conway's text and to one another with narratives elaborating key themes in the book. This can be viewed as a framing and focusing on meaning that is essential to comprehension. However, it can also be viewed, as it was by McVee, as a "narrowing" of focus—a premature assumption of understanding on the part of speakers, such that they gloss over differences in context and meaning in the service of continuity and consensus.

Because their families did not have to grow their own food for the dairy cattle, these speakers did not share Conway's desperate experience of watching livestock starve to death because of drought. McVee, however, experienced this move as one that limited her own and others' opportunity to learn from the narratives by means of comparison and contrast. She grew up on a ranch in Montana. Its isolation, expansiveness, and dependence on climate closely resembled Conway's description of Coorain. Like Conway, McVee lived through her family's near loss of its land because of drought. She viewed the prevailing interpretation as limiting the ways Conway's work might be understood and wanted the group to acknowledge that, in her words, "a ranch is not a dairy farm."

One can imagine other, similar problems with book club discussion—for example, who readings of Conway's book might be undertaken by city dwellers whose sole experience with agriculture was a small window garden. The point is not to assert one "correct" reading of the metaphor but to suggest that the narratives we read—and the narrative responses participants made to them—were not in inherently instructive about difference and diversity. They could be strung together thematically to suggest connection and shared knowledge or they might be read in terms of their difference, thus shedding light on difference in participants' experiences, prior knowledge, or social position. Lack of awareness of these possibilities limits the educative potential of narratives.

Most of us have experienced this kind of conversation. Some of us have, like McVee, opted for silence. Some of us may have tried to voice a different view only to be dismissed or, more insidiously, had our dissent incorporated into the rolling snowball of "I know what you mean." Mostly, we have left these conversations, believing not only that we have understood one another but also that we have understood the author. In short, we have attained the veneer of cooperation and consensus. Yet, to the extent that we have not examined our own differences (and thereby surfaced differences in our readings of the text under discussion), we have not even broached an examination of culture or diversity. The single workshop or the lone foundations course cannot sustain the contact with ideas needed to "turn the soul"—that is, in Haroutunian-Gordon's (1998) terms, to push our thinking and make our discussion not merely sociable, but interpretive. In fact, our glossing of experience in the name of reflection and literature discussion has mostly served to reinforce the entering knowledge and beliefs of each participant (Smyth, 1992). Our tidy, bounded conversation reassures us that we "covered" culture. Yet, if we were to we look closely at our experience we might discover that we have, in fact, failed to *un*cover it.

## UNCOVERING CULTURE

In the Literary Circle, after months of conversation and a receding of the teacher role, we began to find that participants engaged difference and difficult topics and grew to sustain them over time and text. At the beginning of our project, what was particularly evident in participants' talk was a sense of "culturelessness." One teacher said in a debriefing interview after a year of participation, "I was one of those people in the beginning who [thought] I had no culture. There's nothing to me. I've had no experiences." This comment resonates with work in the field of cultural studies, which asserts that members of the so-called "dominant culture" hold taken-for-granted assumptions of an amorphous monoculturalism (Frankenberg, 1993), and a stance of "color blindness"(Paley, 1979/1989). This social positioning limits their reflection on and discussion of race, racism, privilege, and Whiteness (MacIntyre, 1997).

Along with this stance comes what Toni Morrison describes as an informal, unspoken "code of ethics" that denotes how the topic of race should be engaged in public spaces. "In matters of race," Morrison (1992) observes, "silence and evasion have historically ruled" discourse (p. 9). In analyzing the Literary Circle's conversations, particularly those about African-American authors and their texts, we found evidence of this silence around race. We also found evidence that, over time and by means of intertextual experiences, participants were gradually more willing to engage and sustain the topic as they became familiar with one another, book club as an activity, and diverse authors and texts.

The autobiographical literature we read (and the personae of its diverse authors) was a persistent reminder of these topics. And, in the case of some authors like Maya Angelou, the author was a ubiquitous figure in American popular as well as literary culture, whose voice continued to insinuate itself into the group. Participants had what Glazier et al. (2000) called, "Maya sightings" on television, in books, on the radio, and in newspapers. These sightings built a sense of kinship with Angelou, and they began to evoke her and some of the more difficult themes her book address. In addition, as the hot lava of race accumulated in the other books and authors read over the 2 years of the Literary Circle's life span, it became more difficult to avoid.

Participants revisited Angelou's writing seeking links to and differences from the writing of other African-American female authors (e.g., Zora Neale Hurston, Toni Morrison, and Alice Walker; African-American male authors (e.g., James McBride), as well as authors, both male and female, from other times, places, and ethnic groups (e.g., Amy Tan, Mike Rose, Jung Chang, Esmeralda Santiago, Frank McCourt, Mary Crow Dog, and Victor Villasenor). This intertextual reading about hot lava themes such as racism and inequality increased our fluency with ideas and with one another. We began to feel safer to speak—even if that speaking was halting, awkward, or revealing of our own inheritance of racism.

Our conversation and reading across texts shed light on within-group differences, intergroup similarities and differences, and the importance of both local and historical context. It led us beyond stereotyped readings of isolated books, seeking, instead the thematic connections among books and the way taking multiple passes at an idea could increase our understanding of that idea as well as our ability to sustain difficult talk about it. The group began to draw comparisons and contrasts. It was easier for us to examine the historical, social, and political dimensions of oppression in distant societies and cultures such as China than in familiar ones like our own. Reading *Wild Swans*, for example, we were easily and deeply moved by the author's account of the damaging effects oppressive political systems had on the Chinese family. Using descriptions of more distant lives and places as touchstones, we re-read Zora Neale Hurston's *Our Eyes Were Watching God* in a different way. This time we did not focus on gender inequality isolated from or to the exclusion of racism. Instead, having learned from Chang's recounting of these as interwoven in Chinese history, we tackled the more difficult task of considering (and reconsidering) racism's impact on individual and family identity much closer to our hearts and homes.

Our fieldwork suggests that this willingness to risk did not, however, come easily or quickly. *It took 2 years.* Only with sufficient time to negotiate a shared identity as members of the book club did participants appear to break their silence and create for themselves a new "curriculum" for thinking and speaking about what, for White and middle-class Americans, are historically difficult topics. This finding is important and speaks to the forms and functions of teacher professional development in the area of culture.

Professional development in the area of cultural diversity is an act that is notoriously challenging, both because it is difficult for teachers to talk about the aforementioned hot lava topics and because most in-service education is of short duration. Time limits both context and text such that teachers typically learn about "others" by studying the characteristics of ethnic groups in texts (both oral and written) where expert knowledge is presented to them. Lacking opportunities to explore culture as a complex and lived process in which also to participate, and lacking time to garner cultural understanding in and through multiple and complex, multivoiced texts, teachers tend to come away from such professional development reinforced in their extant beliefs and prejudices (McDiarmid & Price, 1990). What seems needed is not multicultural education as a set of techniques or discrete factual content, but as a process of critical engagement—with self, others, texts, and ideas (Chavez Chavez & O'Donnell, 1998).

## EXTENSIONS TO PRACTICE IN TEACHING AND TEACHER EDUCATION

We found extensions into participants' practice in the following forms: curriculum development for pupils; annotated bibliography, teacher support networks, increased collaboration within the research team and attendant growth in friendships among smaller numbers of participants across the lines of differing professional roles. Participants went public about the group, sharing with colleagues what was being learned within it. Finally, we saw a growing interest among the group members to track and document their own learning within this experience—both to enhance their understanding of what has been happening to them and to learn how this experience might be shared with other teachers and with pupils in productive ways. These sorts of learning experiences tend not readily to be available to teachers in their ordinary work and/or staff development; yet they resemble the higher order learning experiences teachers are expected to cultivate in youngsters.

By introducing new forms of talk and new literatures into the study of teaching, we are trying to transform both immediate practice, and the profession's history. As Shotter (1993) pointed out, what is internalized in this model is not only higher order thinking about content, but also norms and values. Both, in my view, are potentially transformative of teacher education if we make communities of learners within teacher education who value democratic participation in learning and are willing to engage lives different from their own.

However necessary it is to change texts and contexts, ultimately we need to recruit and retain a more diverse teaching cohort. Yet, as Galindo and Olguin (1998), who studied Chicana teacher candidates' narratives, pointed out, it is foolish to recruit diverse teachers and then crunch them through the prevailing model of professionalism so that, in they end, they are hardly distinguishable from their more "mainstream" peers. We need instead a professional whose discourse is transforming and transformative, a discourse that can and indeed must incorporate many voices and many sources of knowledge in its construal of what it means to teach, to learn, to be a literate citizen. Following a model of sustained teacher learning rooted in thoughtful dialogue and literature, we might transform teacher knowledge and the forums for sharing it in preservice and continuing education. This transformation might nurture teaching as cultural practice in ways that help us both to recruit and retain a more diverse teaching cohort in the 21st century and also help the teachers who will get us to that goal to work with more insight and efficacy.

# CHAPTER **10**

# How Culture Matters

The illness and death of my mother and father bracket the writing of this book. In the 4 years I worked on it, the passing of my parents heightened my awareness and appreciation of the power of story to create and recreate us. And it is precisely that power I found in the book clubs in which my colleagues and I participated and studied. Most significantly, it was the experience of finding one's "self" in a story—and of discovering that stories of self do not so much reinforce as they construct who we are—and who others are to us. And so, in that spirit, I end this book with an examination of the transformative power of personal narrative, one that draws both on my own family's stories and on the published autobiographies read and discussed in our book clubs.

## MY FATHER'S STORY

In the early 1940s, my father, Frank, and his twin brother, Vincent, lived in a two-family house in urban New Jersey. Except for the incessant chatter of Nana's radio, Italian was heard almost exclusively downstairs in their grandparents' rooms. But upstairs, where the twins lived with their older sister and U.S.-born parents, English was spoken as much as possible. My father recalls his mother insisting that even Nana's fat, pampered cat, which moved easily upstairs and down, be addressed in English by the children. And he jokes that the old mouse-chaser was the only member of the household fully capable of comprehending (and ignoring) commands in both languages.

Sons of a striving father who learned accounting in night school and worked his way into an office job in New York City, the boys were expected to succeed in school. Like the teachers in the neighboring public school attended by my mother, the nuns who taught Frank and Vincent took their charge to socialize immigrant offspring seriously. They taught English with a fervor almost equivalent to that with which they taught the catechism. Standing stark still beside their desks, students were admonished to recite with hands at their sides. Thus, my father learned to temper his Mediterranean expansiveness even as he learned to answer ultimate questions such as, "Why did God make me?" The social pressure to "fit" an American persona shows in photographs taken of the twins during high school. Posing stiffly in matching three-piece suits, they smile weakly at the camera. Buttoned down and slicked back, they look for all the world like what my great grandfather would have called, disparagingly, "Mediganes."

For awhile, Frank and Vincent managed to keep home and school, upstairs and down, comfortably separate. But inevitably these worlds collided. One day, as they crossed the schoolyard with their class en route to Mass, their maternal grandfather, Vincenzo, who was walking in the neighborhood, spotted the twins. Forty years prior, he emigrated from Positano, a poor but beautiful town near Naples. He earned enough money as a produce vendor to marry, bring his wife to the United States, raise a family, and buy a small multiunit house—all without benefit of formal education or English fluency. Vincenzo was a proud, successful man. Adding to his pride was the birth of twin grandsons. They were now fine young men, and he was delighted to see them walking with their class. He waved and called a loud greeting in Italian. Deeply embarrassed, the twins looked the other way and did not return the greeting. They did not want their classmates to see them acknowledge the old man or his language. It was their first and only betrayal of their grandfather, and although Vincenzo never mentioned it to the boys, my father never forgot it.

By the mid-1950s, when my father told me this story, his brother was dead, a casualty of World War II. My father was now part of the thriving post-war middle class. He learned electronics in the Army Air Corps, attended technical school with tuition funded by the GI Bill, and purchased a home in the suburbs with the help of a veteran's mortgage. An engineer in the young field of television, he wished similar opportunities for his children and stressed the central role of education in our success. He did not tell me the story of slighting his grandfather in order to critique the educational system in which I was enrolled. On the contrary, he personalized it, a regretful account of losing sight of the importance of family and letting his grandfather down.

The moral I believe my father wanted me to draw was not that schools should respect language and cultural diversity, but that I should respect my family and not betray its members even while pursuing the goal of education. But the story troubles me 40 years later for several reasons. First, in his account of dishonoring Vincenzo, my father assumes full responsibility without comment on the powerful social forces at work such that his behavior might have "made sense" in its context. Second, the events in his narrative portray education as a painfully double-edged process where the learner must risk alienation from family in order to cross what Soliday (1994) calls the "threshold of possible intellectual, social, and emotional development" (p. 511).

For the children and grandchildren of the great wave of southern European immigrants, stories like this one are plentiful. Others more prominent than my father have turned theirs to art. The film "Big Night," for example, personified immigrant experience in a conflict between two Italian brothers who run a small restaurant in a New Jersey city in the early 1950s. Primo is a brilliant chef, newly arrived and living with his more assimilated younger brother, Secondo, who manages the restaurant and helps in the kitchen. But the restaurant is dying. There is little taste among the American post-war bourgeoisie for Primo's authentic, meticulous regional cooking. In one telling and humorous scene a customer eyes Primo's delicately seasoned seafood risotto with disappointment and asks if it comes with a side of spaghetti.

Secondo implores his brother to compromise and expand the menu, meeting and educating American diners in some sort of gastronomic "zone of proximal development." But Primo is steadfast. He does not want to dilute his recipes, his language, or his identity. Ultimately, the brothers are reduced to wrestling on the Atlantic beachfront. They struggle about who they are, whether to go or stay, how to be Italian in America. Hanging in the balance is the fate of their restaurant, called, not subtly, "Paradise." Paralyzed by conflict, they are outdone by a more savvy neighbor who runs a large and successful establishment catering to the American taste for steak, bland red sauce, cherries jubilee, and tacky renditions of "O Sole Mio."

I don't need to tell you that Paradise is lost in the brothers' struggle (Strum, 1996). But I must also mention that another paradise has, perhaps, been found—albeit briefly. That paradise is visible in the "big night" for which the film is named—a finale of the brother's restaurant at which their finest native cuisine is served to a colorful assortment of new friends and neighbors. Like the meal, this assortment is far from homogenized. It is no mere melting pot. It is a feast. And although "home" is many places and has many meanings to those assembled, it comes together and to life in a working-class restaurant in New Jersey. I return to this possibility of the reorienting of ourselves to paradise later in this chapter.

## THE PROBLEM OF OUR STORIES

Taken at face value, my father's story and the story of the demise of Primo and Secondo's restaurant are quintessentially modern in structure and stance (Bhabha, 1994; McLaren, 1992). They depend for their dramatic action on conflict between groups. Moreover, that conflict is framed and resolved in ways reinforcing the status quo social order. Similarly, Wax (1993) observes a modern preference for representing "culture" as a system of groups, "plural, separate, distinct, (and) historically homogeneous" (p. 108). But he advances two alternative, perhaps more foundational, views. One stresses diffusion of ideas, and culture as created by people in contact. The other, from horticulture, sees culture as the nurturing of growth. As such, like the growth of plants, human development in the context of culture happens in the messy and indeterminate "humus" of our encounters and our conversations over time, place, role, institution, history, and relationship. And, like humus, the precise social constituents or processes of "culture" are difficult to pinpoint (Florio-Ruane & de Tar, 1995; Logan, 1994).

Wax (1993) argues that, for purposes of social reform, simplifying culture by freezing it in time and place and equating it with discrete nationalities or ethnic groups "gives away the store" (p. 108), placing something called "Western culture" at the center, an organizing premise that limits possibility even in arguments advancing multiculturalism. If we were to explore the latter two definitions, however, we might radically reconfigure our stories. If the center cannot hold, then culture is not a place or a group, but an ongoing process of making meaning in contact with others. Clearly, the stories we choose to tell ourselves about the meaning of "culture" have tremendous personal and societal implications and influence the ways we teach and organize schooling.

Narrative is imposed on the bits and pieces of experience to create a coherent sense of meaning spanning past, present, and future. Our stories can become so deeply sedimented that we lose awareness of them as social constructions. They eventually come to shape rather than illuminate experience (Emihovich, 1995; Lakoff & Johnson, 1980). The Spindlers (1994) note in their work on "cultural therapy" this limiting effect of narrative. In their very continuity-giving properties, our "cultural fictions" (McLaren, 1992, p. 86), can lead us to "assume a single, simple world" (p. 84) without history, perspective, contradiction, struggle, or transformation. Think of my father telling me his cautionary tale. As a master narrative organizing my father's experience, it is a tale not of conflict, but of transgression and shame. Responsibility is *exclusively* his. The Spindlers point out that what is therapeutic in looking at the identity-giving stories we tell ourselves is the realization that they are not only about the personal, but also about the social. As such, they can be retold, revised, negotiated, and misunderstood. Indeed, in the last months of my father's life I had the chance to hear family stories again and realize both the comfort in their predictability of plot and the complexity in their re-telling at a time when my father and I were experiencing profound change. *They were not the same stories.* We must be wary in our current rush to celebrate "narrative" as a way of knowing, to ask, "Who is served by this story?" "How does this story distort, even as it represents?"

When I first heard the story of my father and his brother failing to greet Vincenzo, it made a strong impression on me. Not only *about* him, it was told *by* him, and, as a child, I heard it as cautionary. The positioning of my dad as the responsible party in the transgression against his grandfather reproduces and reinforces social inequality in the very narrating of experience. While underlying my father might have had many other feelings and explanations for his actions (he was, after all, a teenager, and most teens are embarrassed by their elders; moreover, he was acutely aware his family's relative newcomer status in the mostly German immigrant community in which he was schooled), he did not voice them. He did not voice nor did I comprehend the social roots of his shame, the tragic American irony of losing his twin in a war against his grandfather's homeland, or his family's gradual transcendence into the American social and economic mainstream.

Similarly, what can be taken from the film, "Big Night," is that Primo and Secondo destroy their own paradise. They kick sand into each other's eyes, thus embodying full responsibility for their problem and leaving out wider social forces as sources of either conflict or support. The tragedy is not only their loss, but also the fact that this loss is represented to them and to others as *exclusively* theirs. This trope reinforces their standing as outsiders, sadly affirming, in McLaren's (1992) words, that "we actively construct and are constructed by the discourses we embody and the metaphors we enact" (p. 80).

## HISTORICAL BACKGROUND

Why do immigrant stories tend to unfold this way? Is paradise inevitably lost? Must family and individual lives be torn asunder in order to make America? A little history helps here. Psychologist Donald Polkinghorne (1991) suggests that narratives arise out of tension or conflict in experience. Stories are attempts to cope with events that are hard to reconcile one with another. Surely the grand narratives of immigrant experience pervasive in our century arose, at least in part, as a response to crisis. When my great grandfather entered the port of New York in the late 19th century, the United States was experiencing the height of immigration from southern and eastern Europe. Many came from illiterate, peasant backgrounds and spoke little or no English. Most neither shared nor comprehended the values of the new political and economic system they were entering.

Those already living in the United States at the time were understandably threatened by this infusion. Although it is almost unimaginable, more immigrants entered America between 1860 and 1930 than the entire population in 1860 (Rips, 1981). And, having recently endured the Civil War, post-war economic hardship, large-scale urbanization, and the rise of rapid travel and communication, immigrants were far from the only perceived threat to Americans' sense of national stability. As policy historian Cohen (1976) describes, in the latter half of the 19th century, "there developed an acute sense that society was coming unstrung, that common values and cohesive institutions were eroding. This sense of loss powerfully influenced social policy" (p. 554).

Ellis Island's expansive facility for processing immigrants testifies to U.S. efforts to mobilize the power of modern bureaucracy to manage crisis. Another modern response was mass public education intended swiftly and efficiently to prepare throngs of immigrants and their children for citizenship. Greene (1994) writes that the historical mission of public education was to "draw our students (diverse though they might appear to be) into some sort of community" (p. 11). To this end, she notes that "we strove for what Dewey called a sharing of experience, the kind of communication in which learning might begin" (p 11).

Although community was deemed essential to the nation's survival, building it was hardly a gentle process. Because immigrants were viewed as a threat to order, formal education forcefully acted to change rather than incorporate their language, values, or traditions into American life. Ellwood Cubberly, for example, described the mission of public education near the turn of the century as if he were penning a morality play. Immigrants, he wrote,

> Tend to settle in groups . . . and to set up here their national manners, customs, and observances. Our task is to break up these groups or settlements, to assimilate and amalgamate these people as part of our American race, and to implant in their children, as far as can be done, the Anglo Saxon conception of righteousness, law and order, and popular government . . . (Cubberly, 1909, cited in Sleeter & Grant 1993, pp. 15–16).

Entailed in Cubberly's defensive prose is nostalgia for a past simpler, more ordered, and stronger in community than the present—a past that critics argue never really existed (Clifford, 1988; Cohen, 1976; Fischer, 1986; McLaren, 1992). Our national narratives thus tragically weave separation of people into stratified groups into the fabric of our thinking about democracy, community, and education. Despite institutional efforts to mold new communities and replace what Americans believed had been lost to modernity, success was never recognized. There was always a new group of outsiders to fear or transform. Even now, as we begin a new century and live in a world linked by almost instant cyber contact, rapid transportation, and economic interdependence, America retains nostalgia for a simpler past and the accompanying fear that diversity will destroy us.

## TO TELL A NEW STORY

Social critic Bhabha (1994) argues that in contemporary times we need to think beyond narratives of people's origins and focus on those "'in-between spaces" where the self is elaborated (pp. 1–2). Encountering his grandfather while in the presence of his schoolmates posed a problem of identity for my father. For him, as for many of us, in James Clifford's (1988) words, "people and things are increasingly out of place" (p. 8). The interconnectedness of the old man with the push cart and the boy who would ultimately learn to fly an airplane and design and operate television cameras raises complicated, but not insurmountable, problems of narrating contact. Yet stories of transformation at the point of contact remain few and far between in U.S. education.

Study after study finds teacher candidates, for instance, holding durable views of cultural diversity as a problem—and a problem limited to people whose skin color differs from their own or who speak more than one language (Paine, 1990; Tatto, 1996; Zeichner, 1993). Teacher education based on categorizing and generalizing about others reinforces societal tendencies to mourn the loss of community and view school as essentially an agency of assimilation. Moreover, teachers assume their role within institutions forged in the last century, and local efforts at innovation are limited by the existing social architecture of the school (Cuban, 1984). In such contexts, it is difficult to reframe school's mission as one of nurturing the knowledge-transforming possibilities of people's contact with one another.

I first glimpsed the possibility of education at the "point of contact" some time after successfully completing my training and teaching in my own classroom. Working as a research assistant to Frederick Erickson and Jeffrey Shultz, I observed young Italian-American children at home and at school. Well tutored in the narrative of border crossing, I was prepared to find the children navigating a risky passage. There is no doubt I could— and did—narrate aspects of their experience in terms of mismatches between school and home communication. But what my colleagues and I also found, a finding most unexpected and one that has meant more to me as the years go by, was that participants made subtle, local adaptations in their practice as they attempted to engage one another in mathematical problem-solving (Shultz, Florio, & Erickson, 1982). Teacher and children took account of one another and adapted their styles of participation, bridging differences in expectation and prior knowledge in order jointly to solve learning problems. This is an example of what Eisenhart (1995) calls a transforming "story of self." It is a story about people making culture together, reshaping, in their moment-to-moment encounters, their educational histories and futures.

Our favorite personal stories can be life enhancing, but they can also hem us in, preventing our own and others' growth. Revising them can make all the difference. Consider, for example, the power of Toni Morrison's (1992) critical turn when she examines the traditional American literary canon as the response of White people to slavery. Or consider what happens to Richard Rodriguez's (1992) sense of himself and society when, in volume two of his autobiography, he criss-crosses borders of time, place, and nation. The lonely scholarship boy finds relationship, responsibility, and irony. Returning to the theme of grieving, as I have missed my mother and my father, I find it necessary to construct a new rendition of "who I am now." I am learning that the paradoxical process of mourning requires changing the story we tell ourselves about who *we are* even as we repeatedly narrate who *they were*.

"Re-emplotment" is the technical, therapeutic term Polkinghorne (1991) gives to this activity. He says that telling new stories is essential to the healing work of therapy after people have experienced challenging life events. Hoffman's (1989) term for the process is "translation therapy," and she illustrates it in her autobiography, *Lost in Translation*. Early in her book, Hoffman seduces us, playing on our conventional expectations by calling the nostalgic account of her childhood in Poland, "Paradise," and the description of her difficult coming of age in English-speaking North America, "Exile." When I first read this book in the company of the teacher candidates in the Future Teachers' Autobiography Club, these were its most accessible parts. Consistent with our schema for the immigrant experience, we read Eva's journey from Paradise into Exile with a delicious sympathy. Yet we felt oddly resourceless as we witnessed her struggle. Eva was for us what my colleague, Taffy Raphael, calls, a "museum piece."

Abruptly, however, Hoffman unsettled us. She transformed her narrative by adding a third, concluding section titled, "The New World." This is difficult, challenging material. It is what happens after loss. It is the reconciliation of experience, and the hope of rediscovering a sense of self in a decentered world. Returning to Poland as an adult, Eva revisits her remembered life. She is trying to write herself into an understanding of life in two languages and across two societies where she will not be "split by the difference" (p. 274). Neither identity nor home is inevitably fixed. Instead, she writes,

> Dislocation is the norm rather than the aberration in our time, but even in the unlikely event that we spend an entire lifetime in one place, the fabulous diverseness with which we live reminds us constantly that we are no longer the norm or the center, that there is no one geographic center pulling the world together and

glowing with the allure of the real thing; . . . in a de centered world we are
always simultaneously in the center and on the periphery. . . (p. 275)

Hoffman's metaphor is not crossing borders, but triangulating. She
surveys her new world by triangulating past, present, and that "unassimil-
able" part of herself that negotiates meaning within difference. She says,
"it's only coming from the ground up that I can hit the tenor of my own
sensibility, hit home" (p. 276). If we are willing to work with Hoffman to
navigate this narrative turn, we find ourselves entering her experience, not
just observing it. We discover, with her, new ways to map the complexity
of our own lives as teachers and learners.

In our time, such radical re-emplotment is asked not only of individuals, but also of institutions. The international New London Group (1996),
for example, advanced a sweeping program of change to the institution of
public education. Taking current practice as their starting point, they call
for collaboration and dialogue to reform school's functions, curriculum,
and pedagogy. Changing the story of schooling may help to foster the
teaching and learning of new literacies and create, in their words,

a new civility in which differences are used as productive resources and in
which differences are the norm. It is the basis for the postnationalist sense of
common purpose that is now essential to a peaceful and productive global
order. (p. 69)

If our stories of self are to help us reform institutions or build new
communities, we need to be willing to reinvent them, repeatedly and in
the company of others, embracing rather than defending ourselves from
contact. We must replace outworn renditions of "who we are" that, in Toni
Morrison's (1994) words, are "unreceptive to interrogation, cannot form
or tolerate new ideas, shape other thoughts, tell another story, fill baffling
silences" (p. 14). Instead, in our scholarship and our teaching, we must
risk telling new stories in and by many voices.

The many voices and stories we might foster in the education of
teachers and pupils would serve several powerful purposes. First, simply
by airing diverse experiences from different points of view, we might be
able to identify those tacit cultural narratives that presently limit our
actions and our sights. Furthermore, we might be able to look critically at
the new narratives we accumulate, struggling with their adequacy, limitations, biases, and power to educate. Bruner (1996) advocates such telling

and investigation of narrative as a collaborative act conferring on participants a sense of agency.

When we tell, hear, and examine stories of self we are not blindly
operating in terms of tacit master narratives. In the proliferating of narratives of culture we begin to see that culture is not frozen or given, but
made and open to negotiation. Yet because our purpose in this work is one
of education, we must also not be paralyzed by the insight that all narratives are "saturated with stifling power, even those which were organized
for liberty" (Mehan, 1995, p. 248). Rather, as Mehan notes,

> When we understand that meaning is constructed, it does not mean that the
> meaning construction process is inevitably evil or wrong or empty. When we
> realize that the ground under claims to authority is not natural but is contested, it
> does not necessarily follow that *all* claims to authority are groundless. (p. 249)

This is an important insight for teachers who not only enact roles of
authority but who, as practitioners, are daily called to act—even in the
face of and in terms of knowledge that is incomplete, biased, and constructed in "the cloudy medium of language" (Mehan, 1995, p. 249).
Despite this reality, teachers are still called to act. They must engage with
their students in the examination of representations of human experience,
prizing not so much attainment of authoritative knowledge but engagement with others in the lifelong process of coming to know.

## BEGINNING WITH ENGAGEMENT

Recently, I read an essay on curriculum by Cross (1998). An educator who
came of age in the segregated south, she recalls a sense of agency and
empowerment in learning that is decidedly absent in the experiences of
the teachers whom she educates today. The mentor Cross remembers
linked academic learning to freedom and to creating a more just and
humane society. Cross does not tell us much more about this teacher,
except that she clearly defied conventional assumptions. Perhaps her
background was responsible for her passion, perhaps her training, perhaps
also the conditions of her work. In the schools for which teachers are currently prepared, that passionate connection between learning and community is at best muffled. Isolated focus on technique combined with the
press to enhance students' performance in high-stakes tests atomizes and
sterilizes the educational experience. We teach by systems; we teach sub-

ject matter; we teach individuals to achieve individually. Where is the Eros in such work—the passionate and powerful dimensions of education that nurture and sustain teachers and learners in and as communities? Where is the joy that Cross felt in her schooling and her profession?

The book in which Cross' essay is included is called, *Speaking Unpleasant: The Politics of (Non)Engagement in the Multicultural Terrain* (Chavez Chavez & O'Donnell, 1998). This collection—and the metaphor on which it is premised—locates a major problem in teaching and teacher education in the difficulty educators have coming to terms with their own biases and perspectives and coming to learn about these in dialogue with others whose backgrounds differ from their own. Other scholars have talked about the difficulty of these tasks with the similar metaphors: King (1991) speaks of the "dysconsciousness" of White teachers toward issues of race; Paley (1979/1989) talks of the allure of a safe "color-blindness." And Morrison (1992) writes that race is an "unspeakable" topic in U.S. society. How do we learn to speak the unspeakable or see what we conscientiously deny? And what would move us to try? Surely it would not be an administrator's exhortation to work harder to achieve higher test scores. It might not even be a stressed and worried parent wondering if we were doing all we might to help a child learn to read. And probably it would not be a professor's urging that we assume a sense of guilt for our share of responsibility for racism.

What would invite such a conversation in and through difficulty would be a sense of passionate engagement, a sense that such conversation would be worth its risks. For contemporary teachers, this seems perhaps a harder sell than it was for teachers like Cross, who came of age during the Civil Rights Movement's apogee. Absent wider social and cultural support for asking difficult questions and having difficult conversations about race or gender or poverty or language diversity, it is easy for us to operate in the default mode, teaching as we remember being taught, thus limiting the educational conversation to one about the means and ends of measurable academic achievement. My hunch is that we do not get very far by asking Euro-American teachers to have difficult conversations when they see no ways to be personally transformed by the experience.

If teaching practice does not provide space for teachers to lead in this transformation, engagement is apt to be low, indeed. Such educational experiences seem to be of the "take your medicine" variety and offer very little in the way of "taking action." They overwhelm and give a sense of hopelessness in the face of a career that will demand action of them. Students in my own institution often resist such experiences—at best, they are trips into the irrelevant or the "exotic," offering stereotyped information about ethnic groups. At worst, they are silencing, self-effacing experiences of what some of the undergraduates I ha' e met call "Guilt 101." They do no see such learning as life enhancing—for themselves or for the children and families they hope to serve as teachers.

To be a learner about self and other in ways that foster transformation is quite a different matter. Both the "I" and the "thou" are changed—enriched—in such encounters. We are moved, inspired, compelled not only by that content of those conversations, but by the very possibility of having them. Nieto (1994) calls this the development of a "caring loyalty" for one another despite all that makes the conversation difficult. Out of such encounters, we do not necessarily achieve consensus, but we create new understandings and, perhaps, new relationships and activities.

Philosopher Henry McHenry (1997), following the work of Martin Buber, illustrates the powerful knowledge that can be created out of "sharing" or "being together" with another person with a modest but joyful example. Writing in his garret, McHenry overhears his young son playing in the rain and is moved to go outside to greet him. McHenry darts across the yard separating the out building where his study is located to meet his young son, dripping, on the porch of his house. Seeing his father, the youngster excitedly "blurts":

> "I don't know what came over me—I was just running and running around like crazy in the yard...!" "*I* know," I said. "What?" He asked breathlessly. *"Rain-running happiness."*

The author continues,

> His face erupted in sunshine, suffused with joy and satisfaction; and I saw in his eye, heard in his voice, the recognition of our secret, exuberant affinity. Where did the moment come from? . . . Though I am the parent, I have no sense that anything I did, consciously or not, caused that moment of what really was heart-stopping communion. I did not tell my child about rain-running happiness; I taught him. We invented rain-running happiness together. How was that moment, a gift to both of us, brought forth? (pp. 341–342).

This example challenges our ordinary assumptions about teaching, learning, and knowledge. It blurs the distinctions between more and less experienced "others," and presents learning as a process of jointly creating knowledge within the momentary encounter in the context of an ongoing relationship. As such, it resembles moments of the collective construction of knowledge that can occur between ethnographers and "informants" after periods of extended contact. There are moments when the struggle to understand one another yields to shared insight.

The identities of ethnographer and informant blur, and together they come to know something they did not know before. Deep knowledge about culture comes out of this contact. Yet the idea of the transactional nature of knowledge about culture was resisted for a long time in anthropology as an undisciplined act of "going native." So powerful were the sanctions against it that one of the most compelling accounts of fieldwork and the intersubjective relationship of researcher and informants, *Return to Laughter*, was published as a memoir rather than an ethnographic monograph and under the anthropologist author's *nom de plume* (Bowen, 1954). In Tedlock's (1991) analysis, the concern over "going native" was "the logical construction of the relationship between objectivity and subjectivity, between scientist an native, between Self and Other, as an unbridgeable opposition" (p. 71).

However, the opposing of self and other in the name of scientific rigor ironically limits what a student of culture can learn. Citing recent ethnographies in which this opposition is rejected, Tedlock notes a recent shift in methodology from "participant observation" to "observant participation"—a shift in both the means and focus of ethnographic analysis and in the ways research is reported. In observant participation, cultural understanding depends on the development of a culture in common in which informant and ethnographer create knowledge together. As such, it relies on extended engagement and reports on the experiences of both the informant and the researcher. A truly "blurred genre" (Geertz, 1983), contemporary cultural study has links to history, memoir, and fiction, as well as to scientific argument. Of this work Tedlock (1991) says, that ethnography's necessary

> communicative interaction, or "we-talk," belongs neither to the realm of objectivity nor to that of subjectivity, but rather to "human intersubjectivity." It is this realm that distinguishes the human sciences from the natural sciences as a field of investigation. (p. 71)

Such a shift in the ways we think about teacher, learner, and knowledge informs and potentially transforms teacher education, particularly as teachers learn about culture. It also challenges our assumption that the knowledge teachers "need"—in this case about culture or power or inequality—is "out there" for the taking. How can we change the terms of the conversation about culture so that it is empowering of teachers rather than alienating of them? What in the teacher's work makes it worth risking sustained, intimate contact with unfamiliar or challenging ideas and interlocutors? Can we hold difficult conversations in which teachers participate joyfully as co-creators of knowledge? We need to be up to this task.

# References

Alba, R. D. (1990). *Ethnic identity: The transformation of white America*. New Haven: Yale University Press.

Anderson-Levitt, K. (2001). *Teaching cultures: Knowledge of teaching first grade in France and the U.S.* Cresskill, NJ: Hampton Press.

Angelou, M. (1969). *I know why the caged bird sings*. New York: Bantam.

Angelou, M. (1974). *Gather together in my name*. New York: Bantam.

Applebee, A. N. (1990). *Literature instruction in American schools* (Report Series 1.4). Albany: Center for the Learning and Teaching of Literature, State University of New York at Albany.

Aries, E. (1976). Interaction patterns and themes in male, female, and mixed gender groups. *Small Group Behavior, 7*(1), 7–19.

Athanases, S. (1998). Diverse learners, diverse texts: Exploring identity and difference through literary encounters. *Journal of Literacy Research, 30*(2), 273–296.

Au, K.H. (1995). Multicultural perspectives on literacy research. *Journal of Reading Behavior, 27*(1), 85–100.

Bakhtin, M. M. (1986). *Speech genres and other late essays*. Austin, TX: University of Texas Press.

Ballenger, C. (1999). *Teaching other people's children: Literacy and learning in a bilingual classroom.* New York: Teachers College Press.

Banks, J. A. (1993, June/July). The canon debate, knowledge construction, and multicultural education. *Educational Researcher,* pp. 4–14.

Barolini, H. (1985). *The Dream Book: An anthology of writings by Italian American women* (First edition). New York: Schocken Books.

Bateson, M.C. (1990). *Composing a life.* New York: Penguin.

Bauman, R. (1986). *Story, performance, and event: Contextual studies of oral narrative.* Cambridge: Cambridge University Press.

Beach, R. (1993). *A teachers' introduction to reader-response theories.* Urbana, IL: National Council of Teachers of English.

Behar, R. (1993). *Translated woman: Crossing the border with Esperanza's story.* Boston: Beacon Press.

Behar, R., & Gordon, D.A. (Eds.) (1995). *Women writing culture.* Berkeley: University of California Press.

Belenky, M. F., Clinchy, B. M., Goldberger, N. R., & Tarule, J. M. (1986). *Women's ways of knowing.* New York: Basic Books.

Belluomini, M. (1985) The dream. In H. Barolini (1985). (Ed.). *The Dream Book: An anthology of writings by Italian American women* (First edition). New York: Schocken.

Bhabha, H. K. (1994). *The location of culture.* London: Routledge.

The Book Club *Plus* Group. (1999). What counts as teacher research? *Language Arts* (Vol. 77, No. 1, pp. 48–53).

Bowen, E.S. (1954). *Return to laughter.* New York: Harper.

Boyle-Baise, M. (1997). Crossing borders to re-think multicultural teacher education. *Curriculum and Teaching, 12*(1), 15–30.

Britton, J. (1982). Spectator role and the beginnings of writing. In M. Nystrand (Ed.), *What writers know* (pp. 149–169). New York: Academic Press.

Britzman, D. (1986). Cultural myths in the making of a teacher: Biography and social structure in teacher education. *Harvard Educational Review, 56*(4), 442–456.

Britzman, D. (1992). The terrible problem of knowing thyself: Toward a poststructural account of teacher identity. *Journal of Curriculum Theorizing, 9*(3), 23–46.

Brooks, C. (1947). *The well-wrought urn: Studies in the structure of poetry.* New York: Harcourt, Brace, & World.

Bruner, J. (1974). The ontogenesis of speech acts. *Journal of Child Language, 2,* 1–19.

Bruner, J. (1996). *The culture of education.* Cambridge, MA: Harvard University Press.

Burbules, N. C. (1993). *Dialogue in teaching: Theory and practice.* New York: Teachers College Press.

Butt R. L., & Raymond, D. (1987). Arguments for using qualitative approaches in understanding teacher thinking: The case for biography. *Journal of Curriculum Theorizing, 7*(1), 62–93.

Calkins, L. (1991). *Living between the lines.* Portsmouth, NH: Heinemann.

Carver, R. (1982). What we talk about when we talk about love. In *What we talk about when we talk about love* (pp. 137–154). New York: Vintage.

Casella, R. (1999). What are we doing when we are "doing" cultural studies in education—and why? *Educational Theory 46*(1), 107–123.

Casey, K. (1993). *I answer with my life: Life histories of women teachers working for social change.* London: Routledge.

Cazden, C. B. (1974). Functions of language in the classroom: Two reviews and a reply. *Research in the Teaching of English, 8,* 60–65.

Cazden, C. B. (1986). Classroom discourse. In M. C. Wittrock (Ed.), *Handbook of research on teaching* (3rd ed., pp. 432–463). New York: MacMillan.

Cazden, C. B. (1988). *Classroom discourse.* Portsmouth, NH: Heinemann.

Cazden, C. B. (1999). Foreword. In C. Ballenger, *Teaching other people's children: Literacy and learning in a bilingual classroom* (pp. vii–viii). New York: Teachers College Press.

Cazden, C. B., & Mehan, H. (1989). Principles from sociology and anthropology: Context, code, and classroom. In M. Reynolds (Ed.), *Knowledge base for the beginning teacher* (pp. 47–57). Oxford: Pergamon.

Chang, J. (1991). *The wild swans.* New York: Doubleday.

Chavez Chavez, R., & O'Donnell, J. (Eds.). (1998). *Speaking the unpleasant: The politics of (non) engagement in the multicultural education terrain.* Albany: State University of New York Press.

Chernin, K. (1994). *In my mother's house.* New York: Harper Perennial.

Cherryholmes, C. (1988). *Power and criticism: Post structural investigations in education.* New York: Teachers College Press.

Clandinnin, J., & Connelly, F. M. (1987). Teachers' personal practical knowledge: What counts as 'personal' in studies of the personal. *Journal of Curriculum Studies, 19*(6), 487–500.

Clark, C. M. (Ed.) (2001). *Talking shop: Authentic conversation and teacher learning.* New York: Teachers College Press.

Clifford, J. (1988). *The predicament of culture: Twentieth-century ethnography, literature and art.* Cambridge, MA: Harvard University Press.

Clifford, J., & Marcus, G. E. (1986). *Writing culture: The poetics and politics of ethnography.* Berkeley: University of California Press.

Coates, J., & Cameron, D. (1989). *Women in their speech communities.* London: Longman.

Cochran-Smith, M. (1991). Learning to teach against the grain. *Harvard Educational Review, 61*(3), 279–310.

Cohen, D. K. (1976). Loss as a theme in social policy. *Harvard Educational Review, 46*(4), 553–571.

Cole, M. (1996). *Cultural psychology: A once and future discipline.* Cambridge, MA: Harvard University Press.

Coles, R. (1989). *The call of stories.* Boston: Houghton Mifflin.

Conle, C. (1997). Between fact and fiction: Dialogue within encounters of difference. *Educational Theory, 47*(2), 181–201.

Conway, J. K. (1989). *The road from Coorain.* New York: Vintage.

Conway, J. K. (Ed.). (1992). *Written by herself: Autobiographies of American women.* New York: Vintage.

Conway, J.K. (1994). *True north.* New York: Random House.

Conway, P. (1998). *Anticipatory reflection while learning to teach: Narratives of hope, fear and expectation.* Unpublished doctoral dissertation, Michigan State University, East Lansing.

Cross, B. (1998). Mediating curriculum: Problems of nonengagement and practices of engagement. In R. Chavez Chavez.& J. O'Donnell (Eds.), *Speaking the unpleasant: The politics of (non) engagement in the multicultural education terrain* (pp. 32–54). Albany: State University of New York Press.

Crow Dog, M. (1990). *Lakota woman.* New York: Harper Perennial.

Cuban, L. (1984). Policy and research dilemmas in the teaching of reasoning: Unplanned designs. *Review of Educational Research, 54,* 655–681.

Cubberly, E. P. (1909). *Changing conceptions of education.* Boston: Houghton Mifflin.

Dasenbrock, R. W. (1992). Teaching multicultural literature. In J. W. Trimmer & T. Warnock (Eds.), *Understanding others: Cultural and cross-cultural studies and the teaching of literature.* Urbana, IL: National Council of Teachers of English.

Davenport, T. H., & Presack, L. (1998). *Working knowledge: How organizations manage what they know.* Boston: Harvard Business School Press.

Davidson, D. (1986). A nice derangement of epitaphs. In E. LePore (Ed.), *Truth and interpretation: Perspectives on the philosophy of Donald Davidson* (pp. 433–446). Oxford: Blackwell.

Davies, B, & Harre, R. (1990). Positioning: The discursive production of selves. *Journal for the Theory of Social Behavior, 20*(1), 43–63.

DeLillo, D. (1997). *Underworld.* New York: Scribner.

Delpit, L. (1995). *Other people's children: Cultural conflict in the classroom.* New York: The New Press.

Denyer, J., & Florio-Ruane, S. (1995). Mixed messages and missed opportunities: Moments of transformation in learning to teach about text. *International Journal of Teaching and Teacher Education, 15*(6), 539–551.

Dewey, J. (1938). *Experience and education.* New York: Collier.

Didion, J. (1979). *The white album.* New York: Simon & Schuster.

di Leonardo, M. (1984). *The varieties of ethnic experience: Kinship, class, and gender among California Italian-Americans.* Ithaca, NY: Cornell University Press.

Duesterberg, L.M. (1998). Rethinking culture in the pedagogy and practices of preservice teachers. *Teaching and Teacher Education, 14*(5), 497–512.

Dressman, M. (1998). Confessions of a methods fetishist: Or, the cultural politics of reflective nonengagement. In R. Chavez Chavez & J. O'Donnell (Eds.), *Speaking the unpleasant: The politics of (non) engagement in the multicultural terrain* (pp. 108–126). Albany: State University of New York Press.

Dyson, A. H., & Genishi, C. (Eds.). (1994). *The need for story: Cultural diversity in classroom and community.* Urbana, IL: National Council of Teachers of English.

Edelsky, C. (1993). Who's got the floor? In D. Tannen (Ed.), *Gender and conversational interaction* (pp. 189–227). New York: Oxford University Press.

Eeds, M. W., & Wells, D. (1989). Grand conversations: An exploration of meaning construction in literature study groups. *Research in the Teaching of English, 23,* 4–29.

Eisenhart, M. (1995). The fax, the jazz player, and the self-story teller: How do people organize culture? *Anthropology and Education Quarterly, 26*(1), 3–26.

Elbow P. (1986). *Embracing contraries: Explorations in learning and teaching.* New York: Oxford University Press.

Emihovich, C. (1995). Distancing passion: Narratives in social science. In J. Wisniewski & R. Hatch (Eds.), *Life history and narrative* (pp. 37–48). London: The Falmer Press.

Erickson, F. (1996). On the evolution of qualitative approaches in educational research: From Adam's task to Eve's. *Australian Educational Researcher 23*(2), 1–15.

Erickson, F., & Shultz, J. (1975). When is a context? Some issues of theory and method in the analysis of social competence. *Quarterly Newsletter of the Institute for Comparative Human Development, 1*(1), 5–10.

Ferdman, B. (1990). Literacy and cultural identity. In M. Minami & B. P. Kennedy (Eds.), Language *issues in literacy and bilingual/multicultural edu-*

*cation* (Vol. Reprint Series, No. 22, pp. 347–371). Cambridge, MA: Harvard Educational Review.

Ferdman, B. (1991). Becoming literate in a multiethnic society. In A. Purves (Ed.), *Literate systems and individual lives: Perspectives on literacy and schooling* (pp. 95–115). Albany: State University of New York Press.

Finnan, C., & Swanson, J. D. (2001). *Accelerating the learning of all students: Cultivating culture change in schools, classrooms, and individuals.* Boulder, CO: Westview.

Fish, S. (1980). *Is there a text in this class? The authority of interpretive communities.* Cambridge, MA: Harvard University Press.

Fischer, M. (1986). Ethnicity and the post-modern arts of memory. In J. Clifford & G. E. Marcus (Eds.), *Writing culture: The poetics and politics of ethnography* (pp. 194–223). Berkeley: University of California Press.

Florio-Ruane, S. (1989). Social organization of classes and schools. In M. Reynolds (Ed.), *Knowledge base for the beginning teacher* (pp. 163–177). Oxford: Pergamon.

Florio-Ruane, S., & Raphael, T. E. (2001). Reading lives: Creating and sustaining learning about culture and literacy education in teacher study groups. In C. M. Clark (Ed.). (2001). *Talking shop: Authentic conversation and teacher learning.* New York: Teachers College Press.

Florio-Ruane, S., & McVee, M. (2000). Ethnographic approaches to literacy research. In M. Kamil, R. Barr, P. D. Pearson, & P. Mosenthal (Eds.), *Handbook of reading research* (4th ed., pp. 153–162). Mahwah, NJ: Lawrence Erlbaum Associates.

Florio-Ruane, S., Raphael, T. E., Glazier, J., McVee, M., & Wallace, S. (1997). Discovering culture in discussions of autobiographical literature: Transforming the education of literacy teachers. In C. K. Kinzer, K. A. Hinchman, & D. J. Leu (Eds.), *Inquiries into literacy theory and practice (Forty-sixth handbook of the National Reading Conference)* (pp. 452–464). Chicago: The National Reading Conference.

Florio-Ruane, S., & deTar, J. (1995). Conflict and consensus in teacher candidates' discussion of ethnic autobiography. *English Education, 27*(1), 11–39.

Florio, S., & Walsh, M. (1981). The teacher as colleague in classroom research. In H. T. Trueba, G. P. Guthrie, & K. H. Au (Eds.), *Culture and the bilingual classroom* (pp. 87–101). Rowley: Newbury House.

Forster, E.M. (1921). *Howard's end.* New York: Random House.

Frankenberg, R. (1993). *White women, race matters: The social construction of whiteness.* Minneapolis: The University of Minnesota Press.

Freund, E. (1987). *The return of the reader: Reader-response criticism.* London: Methuen.

Galda, L. (1998). Mirrors and windows: Reading as transformation. In T. E. Raphael & K. H. Au (Eds.), *Literature-based instruction: Reshaping the curriculum* (pp. 1–11). Norwood: Christopher-Gordon.

Galindo, R., & Olguin, M. (1998). Reclaiming bilingual educators' cultural resources: An autobiographical approach. *Urban Education, 31*(1), 29–56.

Gavelek, J., & Raphael, T.E. (1996). Changing talk about text: New roles for teachers and students. *Language Arts, 73,* 24–34.

Gay, G. (1993). Building cultural bridges: A bold proposal for teacher education. *Education and Urban Society, 25*(3), 285–299.

Gee, J. P. (1989). *What is literacy?* (Tech. Rep. No. 2). Brookline, MA: The Literacies Institute, Educational Development Corporation.

Geer, B. (1969). First days in the field: A chronicle of research in progress. In G. McCall & J. Simmons (Eds.), *Issues in participant observation* (pp. 144–162). Reading, MA: Addison Wesley.

Geertz, C. (1983). *Local knowledge: Further essays in interpretive anthropology.* New York: Basic Books. Geertz, C. (1973). *The interpretation of cultures.* New York: Basic Books.

Gere, A. R. (1997). *Intimate practices: Literacy and cultural work in U.S. women's clubs, 1880–1920.* Urbana: University of Illinois.

Gernes, T. (1992). *Recasting the culture of ephemera: Young women's literary culture in nineteenth-century America.* Unpublished doctoral dissertation, Brown University, Providence, RI.

Gilmore, P., & Glatthorn, A. (Eds.). (1982). *Children in and out of school: Ethnography and education.* Washington, DC: The Center for Applied Linguistics.

Glaser, B., & Strauss, A. (1967). *The discovery of grounded theory.* Chicago: Aldine.

Glazier, J., McVee, M., Wallace-Cowell, S., Shellhorn, B., Florio-Ruane, S., & Raphael, T. (2000). Teacher learning in response to autobiographical literature. In N. Karolides (Ed.), *Reader response in secondary and college classrooms* (2nd ed., pp. 287–310). Mahwah, NJ: Lawrence Erlbaum Associates.

Glazier, J. (1997). *Conceptions and context: a broad story of how conceptions of whiteness may influence white women's work in classrooms.* Unpublished manuscript, Michigan State University, East Lansing.

Goffman, E. (1961). *Encounters: Two studies in the sociology of interaction.* New York: Bobbs-Merrill.

Goffman, E. (1974). *Frame analysis.* New York: Harper Colophon.

Goodenough, W.H. (1976). Multi-culturalism as the normal human experience. *Anthropology and Education Newsletter 7*(4), 4–7.

Gordon, R. L. (1980). *Interviewing: Strategies, techniques, and tactics.* Homewood, IL: Dorsey Press.

Grant, C. (1989). *Culture and teaching: What do teachers need to know?* (Conference Series 89–1, Vol. 2). East Lansing: Michigan State University National Center for Research on Teacher Learning.

Greene, M. (1994). Multiculturalism, community, and the arts. In A. H. Dyson & C. Genishi (Eds.), *The need for story: Cultural diversity in classroom and community* (pp. 11–27). Urbana, IL: National Council of Teachers of English.

Griffin, G. A. (1991). Interactive staff development: Using what we know. In A. Lieberman & L. Miller (Ed.), *Staff development in the '90s': New demands, new realities, new perspectives* (pp. 243–260). New York: Teachers College Press.

Grumet, M. (1980). Autobiography and reconceptualization. *Journal of Curriculum Theorizing, 2*(2), 155–158.

Harris, D. L. (1995). *Composing a life as a teacher: The role of conversation and community in teachers' formation of their identity as professionals.* Unpublished doctoral dissertation, Michigan State University, East Lansing.

Haroutunian-Gordon, S. (1998). A study of reflective thinking patterns in interpretive discussion. *Educational Theory, 48*(1), 33–58.

Haroutunian-Gordon, S. (1991). *Turning the soul.* Chicago: University of Chicago Press.

Hartman, D. (1991). The intertextual link of readers using multiple passages: A postmodern/semiotic/cognitive view of meaning making. In J. Zutell & S. McCormick (Eds.), *Learner factors/teacher factors: Issues in literacy research (Fortieth Yearbook of the National Reading Conference)* (pp. 616–636). Chicago: NRC.

Hawkins, D. (1974). I, thou, and it. In D. Hawkins (Ed.), *The informed vision: Essays on learning and human nature* (pp. 48–62). New York: Agathon Press.

Hermans, H. J. M., & Kempens, H. J. G. (1998). Moving cultures: The perilous problems of cultural dichotomies in a globalizing society. *American Psychologist, 53*(10), 1111–1120.

Hoffman, D. (1996). Culture and self in multicultural education: Reflections on discourse, text, and practice. *American Educational Research Journal, 33*(3), 545–569.

Hoffman, E. (1989). *Lost in translation: A life in a new language.* New York: Penguin.

Hoffman, E. (1993). *Exit into history.* New York: Penguin.

Holte, J. C. (1988). *The ethnic I: A sourcebook for ethnic-American autobiography.* New York: Greenwood Press.

Hurston, Z. N. (1937). *Their eyes were watching God*. New York: Harper Perennial.

Hymes, D. (1981). *"In vain I tried to tell you": Essays in Native American ethnopoetics*. Philadelphia: University of Pennsylvania Press.

Hymes, D. (1982). What is ethnography? In P. Gilmore & A. A. Glatthorn (Eds.), *Children in and out of school: Ethnography and education* (pp. 21–32). Washington, DC: Center for Applied Linguistics.

Irvine, J. (1979). Formality and informality in communicative events. *American Anthropologist, 81*(4), 769–790.

Jackson, P. W. (1998). *John Dewey and the lessons of art*. New Haven, CT: Yale University Press.

Jenkins, L., & Kramer, C. (1978). Small group process: Learning from women. *Women's Studies International Quarterly, 1*(1), 67–84.

Jimenez, R., Moll, L., Rodriguez-Brown, F., & Barrera, R. (1999). Conversations: Latina and Latino researchers interact on issues related to literacy learning. *Reading Research Quarterly, 34*(2), 217–230.

Johnson, G. (1997). Reframing teacher education and teaching: From personalism to post-personalism. *Teaching and Teacher Education, 13*(8), 815–829.

Jordan, R. A., & Kalcik, S. J. (Eds.). (1985). *Women's folklore, women's culture*. Philadelphia: University of Pennsylvania Press.

Kailin, J. (1999). Preparing urban teachers for schools and communities: Anti-racist perspectives. *The High School Journal*, pp. 80–87.

Kalcik, S. (1975). ". . . like Ann's gynecologist or the time I was almost raped" Personal narratives in women's rap groups. *Journal of American Folklore, 83*, 3–11.

King, J. (1991). Dysconscious racism: Ideology, identity, and the miseducation of teachers. *Journal of Negro Education, 60*(2), 133–146.

Kozol, J. (1991). *Savage inequalities*. New York: Crown.

Kuchar, M.D. (1999). *The effect of a language mediated apprenticeship on the career maturity and academic achievement of 12th grade minority students*. Unpublished doctoral dissertation, Fordham University, New York.

Labov, W. (1972). *Language in the inner city*. Philadelphia: University of Pennsylvania Press.

Lakoff, G., & Johnson, M. (1980). *Metaphors we live by*. Chicago: The University of Chicago Press.

Landes, R. (1965). *Culture in American education: Anthropological approaches to minority and dominant groups in the schools*. New York: Wiley.

Lave, J., & Wenger, E. (1991). *Situated learning: Legitimate peripheral participation*. Cambridge: Cambridge University Press.

Lentriccia, F., & McLaughlin, T. (1990). *Critical terms for literary study.* Chicago: The University of Chicago Press.

Leacock, E. B. (1971). *The culture of poverty: A critique.* New York: Simon & Schuster.

LePore, E. (Ed.). (1986). *Truth and interpretation: Perspectives on the philosophy of Donald Davidson.* Oxford: Blackwell.

Lieberman, A., & Miller, L. (Eds.). (1991). *Staff development in the '90s: New demands, new realities, new perspectives.* New York: Teachers College Press.

Lionnet, F. (1989). *Autobiographical voices: Race, gender, and self-portraiture.* New York: Cornell University Press.

Logan, W. B. (1994, February 16). What is this strange thing called humus? *The New York Times,* p. 49.

Lortie, D. C. (1975). *Schoolteacher: A sociological study.* Chicago: The University of Chicago Press.

MacIntyre, A. (1997). *Making meaning of whiteness: Exploring racial identity with white teachers.* Albany: State University New York Press.

Marshall, J. D. (1989). *Patterns of discourse in classroom discussions of literature* (Report Series 2.9): Albany, NY: Center for the Learning and Teaching of Literature.

Marshall, J., Smagorinsky, P., & Smith, M. (1995). *The language of interpretation: Patterns of discourse in discussions of literature.* Urbana, IL: National Council of Teachers of English.

McBride, J. (1996). *The color of water.* New York: Riverhead Books.

McCourt, F. (1996). *Angela's ashes.* New York: Scribner.

McDermott, R. P., & Tylbor, H. (1983). On the necessity of collusion in conversation. *Text, 3*(3), 277–297.

McDiarmid, G. W. (1989). *What do prospective teachers learn in their liberal arts courses?* (Issue Paper No. 89–8). East Lansing: Michigan State University National Center for Research on Teacher Learning.

McDiarmid, G. W., & Price, J. (1990). *Prospective teachers' views of diverse learners: A study of participants in the ABCD project* (Research Rep. No. 90–6). East Lansing: National Center for Research on Teacher Education, Michigan State University.

McHenry, H. D. (1997). Education as encounter: Buber's pragmatic ontology. *Educational Theory, 47*(3), 341–357.

McLaren, P. (1992). Collisions with Otherness: "Traveling" Theory, Post-Colonial Criticism, and the Politics of Ethnographic Practice—The Mission of the Wounded Ethnographer. *Qualitative Studies in Education 5*(1), 77–92.

McLaren, P. (1997, Fall). Decentering whiteness: In search of a revolutionary multiculturalism. *Multicultural Education*, pp. 12–15.

McMahon, S. I., & Raphael, T. E., with Goatley, V. J., & Pardo, L. S. (1997). *The Book Club project: Exploring alternative contexts for literacy instruction.* New York: Teachers College.

McVee, M. B. (1999). *Narrative and the exploration of culture, self, and other in teacher's book club discussion groups.* Unpublished doctoral dissertation, Michigan State University, East Lansing.

Mead, G. H. (1956). *On social psychology.* Chicago: University of Chicago Press.

Mehan, H. (1995). Resisting the Politics of Despair. *Anthropology and Education Quarterly 26*(3), 239–250.

Meier, D. (1995). *The power of their ideas: Lessons for America from a small school in Harlem.* Boston: Beacon Press.

Moll, L., & Greenberg, J. B. (1990). Creating zones of possibilities: Combining social contexts for instruction. In L. C. Moll (Ed.), *Vygotsky and education: Instructional implications and applications of sociohistorical psychology* (pp. 319–348). Cambridge: Cambridge University Press.

Morrison, T. (1987). *Song of Solomon.* New York: Penguin.

Morrison, T. (1992). *Playing in the dark.* New York: Vintage.

Morrison, T. (1994). *The Nobel lecture in literature: 1993.* New York: Knopf.

Mukherjee, B. (1989). *Jasmine.* New York: Fawcett Crest.

Nash, R.J. (n.d.). *Teaching philosophy of education as moral conversation: A lengthy memo to my graduate students.* Unpublished manuscript, The University of Vermont, Burlington.

The New London Group. (1996). A pedagogy of multiple literacies: Designing social futures. *Harvard Educational Review, 66*(1), 60–92.

Newman, D., Griffin, P., & Cole, M. (1989). *The construction zone: Working for cognitive change in school.* New York: Cambridge University Press.

Nias, J. (1989). *Primary teachers talking A study of teaching as work.* London: Routledge.

Nieto, S. (1994, Spring). Affirmation, solidarity, and critique: Moving beyond tolerance in multicultural education. *Multicultural Education,* 9–12, 35–38.

O'Connor, M. C., & Michaels, S. (1993). Aligning academic task and participation status through revoicing: Analysis of a classroom discourse strategy. *Anthropology and Education Quarterly, 24*(4), 318–335.

Ogbu, J. (1987). Variability in minority school performance: A problem in search of an explanation. *Anthropology and Education Quarterly, 18*(2), 312–334.

Orenstein, P. (1994). *Schoolgirls: Young women, self-esteem, and the confidence gap.* New York: Doubleday Anchor.

Pailliotet, A.W. (1995). Extending inquiries initiated in the Future Teachers' Autobiography Club. *English Education, 27*(1), 6–10.

Paine, L. (1990). *Orientation towards diversity: What do prospective teachers bring?* (Research Rep. No. 89–9). East Lansing: Michigan State University National Center for Research on Teacher Education.

Paley, V.G. (1995). *Kwanzaa and me: A teacher's story.* Cambridge, MA: Harvard University Press.

Paley, V. (1986). On listening to what the children say. *Harvard Educational Review, 56*(2), 122–131.

Paley, V. G. (1979/1989). *White teacher.* Cambridge, MA: Harvard University Press.

Penuel, W. R., & Wertsch, J. V. (1995). Vygotsky and identity formation: A sociocultural approach. *Educational Psychologist, 30*(2), 83–92.

Phelps, L. W. (1988). *Composition as a human science: Contributions to the self-understanding of a discipline.* New York: Oxford University Press.

Phillion, J. (1999). Narrative and formalistic approaches to the study of multiculturalism. *Curriculum Inquiry, 29*(1), 129–145.

Pike, K. (1967). *Language in relation to a unified theory of the structure of human behavior.* The Hague: Mouton.

Polkinghorne, D. E. (1991). Narrative and self-concept. *Journal of Narrative and Life History, 1* (2&3), 135–153.

Pratt, M. L. (1986). Fieldwork in common places. In J. M. Clifford & G. E. Marcus (Eds.), *Writing culture: The poetics and politics of ethnography* (pp. 27–50). Berkeley: University of California Press.

Probst, R. (1988). *Response and analysis: Teaching literature in junior and senior high school.* Portsmouth, NH: Heinemann.

Proefriedt, W. A. (1989/1990). The immigrant or "outsider" experience as metaphor for becoming an educated person in the modern world: Mary Antin, Richard Wright, and Eva Hoffman. *MELUS, 16*(2), 77–89.

Raphael, T. E., Goatley, V. J., McMahon, S. I., & Woodman, D. A. (1995). Promoting meaningful conversations in student-led book clubs. In N. Roser & M. Martinez (Eds.), *Book talk and beyond* (pp. 71–83). Newark, DE: The International Reading Association.

Raphael, T. E., & Hiebert, E. (1996). *Creating an integrated approach to literacy instruction.* New York: Harcourt Brace.

Reischl, C. (1999). *Beginning and practiced teachers constructing culture.* Unpublished doctoral dissertation, Michigan State University, East Lansing.

Richards, D. A. J. (1999). *Italian American: The racializing of an ethnic identity.* New York: New York University Press.

Rips, G. N. (1981). *Coming to America: Immigrants from southern Europe*. New York: Delacorte.

Rodriguez, R. (1982). *Hunger of memory: The education of Richard Rodriguez*. New York: Bantam.

Rodriguez, R. (1992). *Days of obligation: An argument with my Mexican father*. New York: Penguin.

Rosaldo, R. (1989). *Culture and truth: The remaking of social analysis*. Boston: Beacon Press.

Rose, M. (1989). *Lives on the boundary*. New York: Penguin.

Rose, M. (1995). *Possible lives*. New York: Houghton Mifflin.

Rosen, H. (1985). The autobiographical impulse. In D. Tannen (Ed.), *Linguistics in context: Connecting observation and understanding* (pp. 69–88). Norwood: Ablex.

Rosen, H. (1987). *Stories and meanings*. Sheffield, UK: The National Association for the Teaching of English.

Rothstein, E. (1999, June 17). In a word, culture means anything, bad as well as good. *The New York Times,* pp. B–1, and B–4.

Salvio, P. M. (1990). Transgressive daughters: Student autobiography and the project of self-creation. *Cambridge Journal of Education, 20*(3), 283–289.

Santiago, E. (1993). *When I was Puerto Rican*. New York: Vintage.

Sarroub, L. (2000). Becoming American, remaining Arab: How the "hijabat" negotiate life in two worlds. Unpublished doctoral dissertation, Michigan State University, East Lansing.

Schieffelin, B., & Ochs, E. (1986). *Language socialization across cultures*. Cambridge: Cambridge University Press.

Schubert, W. H. (1991). Teacher lore: A basis for understanding praxis. In C. Witherell & N. Noddings (Eds.), *Stories lives tell: Narrative and dialogue in education* (pp. 207–233). New York: Teachers College.

Schultz, F. (Ed.). (1995). *Annual editions: Multicultural education (95/96)*. Guilford: Dushkin.

Schwab, J. (1976). Education and the state: Learning community. In *Great ideas today* (pp. 234–271). Chicago: Encyclopedia Britannica.

Scribner, S. (1984). Literacy in three metaphors. *American Journal of Education, 93*(1), 7–22.

Shotter, J. (1993). Vygotsky: The social negotiation of semiotic mediation. *New Ideas in Psychology, 11* (1), 61–75.

Shultz, J., Florio, S., & Erickson, F. (1982). Where's the floor? Aspects of the cultural organization of social relationships in communication at home and at school. In P. Gilmore & A. Glatthorn (Eds.), *Children in and out of school: Ethnography and education* (pp. 88–123). Washington, DC: The Center for Applied Linguistics.

Sleeter, C. E. (1994, Spring). White racism. *Multicultural Education,* pp. 5–8, 39.

Sleeter, C. E., & Grant, C.A. (1993). *Making choices for multicultural education: Five approaches to race, class, and gender.* New York: MacMillan.

Smyth, J. (1992). Teachers' work and the politics of reflection. *American Educational Research Journal, 29*(2), 267–300.

Soliday, M. (1994). Translating self and difference through literacy narratives. *College English, 56*(5), 511–526.

Spindler, G., & Spindler, L. (1994). *Pathways to cultural awareness: Cultural therapy with teachers and students.* Thousand Oaks, CA: Sage.

Spiro, R. J., Feltovich, P. J., Jacobson, M. I., & Coulson, R. L. (1993/1995). *Cognitive flexibility, constructivism, and hypertext: Random access instruction for advanced knowledge in ill-structured domains.* ILT/web. Institute for Learning Technologies. *Webmaster@ilt.columbia.edu.*

Spiro, R. J., & Jehng, J. C. (1990). Cognitive flexibility, random access instruction, and hypertext: Theory and technology for the nonlinear and multidimensional traversal of complex subject matter. In D. Nix & R. J. Spiro (Eds.), *Cognition, education, and multimedia* (pp. 163–205). Hillsdale, NJ: Lawrence Erlbaum Associates.

Stahl, S. (1985). *Literary folkloristics and the personal narrative.* Bloomington: Indiana University Press.

Steinberg, S. (1989). *The ethnic myth: Race, ethnicity, and class in America.* Boston: Beacon Press.

Steinbeck, J. (1969). *Journal of a novel: The East of Eden letters.* New York: Penguin.

Stone, A. E. (Ed.). (1981). *The American autobiography: A collection of critical essays.* Englewood, NJ: Prentice-Hall.

Strum, C. (1996, October 27). Garden State? The image is closer to crab grass. *The New York Times,* pp. 33 & 50.

Talese, G. (1993, March 14). Where are the Italian-American novelists? In *The Book Review.* New York: The New York Times, pp. 23–25, 29.

Talese, G., & Lounsberry, B. (1996). *Writing creative non-fiction: The literature of reality.* New York: HarperCollins.

Tan A. (1991). *The kitchen god's wife.* New York: Ballentine Books.

Tannen, D. (Ed.). (1985). *Linguistics in context: Connecting observation and understanding.* Norwood, NJ: Ablex.

Tannen, D. (1989). *Talking voices.* New York: Cambridge University Press.

Tannen, D. (Ed.) (1993). *Gender and conversational interaction.* New York: Oxford University Press.

Tatto, M. T. (1996). Examining values and beliefs about teaching diverse students: Understanding the challenges for teacher education. *Educational Evaluation and Policy Analysis, 18*(2), 155–180.

Tedlock, B. (1991). From participant observation to the observation of participation: The emergence of narrative ethnography. *Journal of Anthropological Research, 47,* 69–94.

Torres-Petersen, M., & John-Steiner, V. (1995, July). *Impediments to teachers' co-construction of educational knowledge: A sociocultural approach.* Paper presented at the 25th Congreso Interamericano de Psicologia, San Juan, Puerto Rico.

Trimmer, J., & Warnock, T. (Eds). (1992). *Understanding others: Cultural and cross-cultural studies and the teaching of literature.* Urbana, IL: NCTE.

Trueba, H. (1989). *Cultural embeddedness: The role of culture in minority students' acquisition of English literacy* (Conference Series 89–1, Vol. 2). East Lansing: Michigan State University National Center for Research on Teacher Learning.

Trueba, H. T., Guthrie, G. P., & Au, K. H. (Eds.). (1981). *Culture and the bilingual classroom.* Rowley: Newbury House.

Van Manen, M. (1977). Linking ways of knowing with ways of being practical. *Curriculum Inquiry, 6,* 205–228.

Villasenor, V. (1991). *Rain of gold.* New York: Delta Books.

Vygotsky, L. (1978). *Mind in society: The development of higher psychological processes.* Cambridge, MA: Harvard University Press.

Walker, A. (1983). *In search of our mothers' gardens.* New York: Harcourt Brace.

Walker, N. T., & MacGillivray, L. (1999). *Latina teachers: Negotiating higher education* (Research Rep.). Ann Arbor: University of Michigan Center for Improvement of Early Reading Achievement.

Wax, M. (1993). How culture misdirects multiculturalism. *Anthropology and Education Quarterly, 24*(2), 99–115.

Welty, E. 1983). *One writer's beginnings.* Cambridge, MA: Harvard University Press.

Wittgenstein, L. (1953). *Philosophical investigations* (3rd ed.). New York: MacMillan.

Wong, S. (1991). Immigrant autobiographies: Some questions of definition and approach. In P. J. Eakin (Ed.), *American autobiography: Retrospect and prospect* (pp. 142–170). Madison: University of Wisconsin Press.

Wortham, S. (1995). Experiencing the great books. *Mind, Culture, and Activity, 2*(2), 66–80.

Zeichner, K. (1993). *Education teachers for cultural diversity* (Tech. Rep.). East Lansing: Michigan State University Center for Research on Teacher Learning.

Zuss, M. (1997). Strategies of representation: Autobiographical metissage and critical pragmatism. *Educational Theory, 47*(2), 163–180.

# Appendix:
# Sample Narratives

## ACQUIRING A SECONDARY DISCOURSE:
## LOSS AND CULTURAL CHANGE[1]

### "Peggy at College"

**P:** He said a lot about this coming home. He starts talking about when he comes home from college and he just can't relate, and I thought about something we talked about last time . . .

**Ma:** Yes, we did, and I talked about my roommate.

**N:** Is that the part where he talks about what he did on the weekend and he doesn't really like to talk about . . .

**P:** Yeah, but he couldn't say it all, and I felt that he couldn't relate to his parents completely. I could understand that and especially having parents that didn't finish college. My dad never began, especially that contrast, that he never

---

[1]Slight editorial changes were made in transcribing these oral narratives. See Paley (1986) for models of both the careful study of student narratives and the method of editing them for readability.

attended any college whatsoever and to try to explain to him is like, I know he's not getting it. I just try to tell him a little bit of what I think he might kind of understand. Not that he can't understand what I'm saying, but that he can't relate to the emotion or the experience. It is really interesting to me, that disconnectedness. You know that, wow; I just made the connection now. You go away to college for the "better life," I mean what we say is a better life. You are starting to succeed. College is success. But what do you lose when you go to college? I know that I lost much closeness with my family and my hometown. I could never return there because of college. My ideas have been transformed so much. I have lost what I have grown up with. I couldn't return to that. I think it is a very narrow-minded place, a prejudiced place, because of who I have become in college and what I've had a chance to, the experiences you feel.

## RESISTANCE AND CULTURAL IDENTITY

### "The Boys in Detroit"

**Ma:** I talk to my dad about this. I am thinking, what if you are an inner city Detroit, 16-year-old Black male, and you want to succeed, want to learn, want to succeed in education to get out of poverty. I guess this is a kind of common thing, but it kind of hit me like a lightening bolt: if I choose one thing that I want, I'm going to be hurt. If I choose the other thing that I want to be: I want to be intimate, I want to live like I have always lived, to enjoy my culture and the things I enjoy in life, I won't have this. It is one or the other. You are isolated.

### "La Toya's Cut-Downs"

**Ja:** I was talking about La Toya who was telling me that you have to give cut-downs to be popular. I kept telling her my values I guess, and she finally told me, "Well, Miss Wilson, this is how I have been since kindergarten. How can I change after all this time?" And, you know I didn't know what to tell her. It seemed like she was almost to the point where she was saying, "I agree with you, but I don't know how to do it. I can't do it." I think she is afraid to say to me . . . I mean she wanted to defend her way.

**P:** It seems to me very much like La Toya definitely had two conflicting . . . well, I wrote in my journal about "what culture?" I think of a classroom culture, adult culture, peer culture, or whatever. A set of norms would be a better word for it, or values. But she is torn between two. If I cross over to what Miss Wilson believes, then I lose friends. If I stay here, the teacher doesn't like me and I'm really messing up discipline-wise, but I have friends. So there is always loss by having to cross over and I don't know, it is.

# GENDER AND CULTURAL IDENTITY

## "Rusha and Waffa"

**M:** In my class there are two girls both of whom are from Saudi Arabia. One has been here since she was seven, and one of them just got here. Rusha has been here for awhile and speaks fluent English. You would think that the girl was born here. She just bops around like everybody else. She is little and does not hesitate to shove the biggest guy in the class out of her way if she wants to get to the computer. And then there is Waffa who comes in, this timeless little face—like the faces you see in paintings. She comes in and is so quiet. She won't talk and is just gentle, very much like the women are in Saudi Arabia because they really don't have that much of a voice there. And here is Mr. Gable saying, "Waffa, talk. We want to hear what you have to say. It is important."

**P:** Can you imagine that's not her culture?

**M:** And she . . . It's not at all. It was so funny one day she was collecting hot lunch envelopes. She said, "(whispering) Everybody, I need your lunch envelopes." And Mr. Gable looked at her because Rachel was running around doing things. So Michael leans over and says, "(whispering) Waffa, nobody is going to hear you if you talk like this. The room's too noisy."

**P:** There's a public and a private voice.

**M:** But Rusha's father is so excited, and I talk about this to Mr. Gable so much, because he keeps saying Rusha is going back soon. I am thinking that when she goes back she is going to be crushed because she is a very independent thinker and a very independent person. Like I said, she would punch people out of the way. If she wants to do something and somebody is goofing around and getting in the way of her success, she is like, "(loudly) Excuse me!" Oh, my goodness, we are saying, she will probably want to come back here. I don't know what is going to happen when she goes back to Saudi Arabia.

**M:** You know, we talk so much about how we want these kids to establish some sort of value system where they are getting some from us and some from home. Somewhere along the line they have some kind of value system, and of course we think it is good if it comes in whatever we do. In our classroom it is very good to share your thoughts and that is something we personally value. It is also valued in this school and in this community—to speak up and say what you think. And Rusha, if you think about it, from first to fourth grade this has been her childhood. This is what she knows. What is supposedly her culture in Saudi Arabia is something she has never grown up in. I just look at that and it is just one of those situations where I just say, "I know that she is a smart girl and I hope it will come out some day."

**P:** What scares me is that we are saying that is good: that you should speak up. But in her culture that is not so. We are imposing our values, I mean I totally agree with that value, but then I think of how it is for her having to go back home. Not only does she have to switch over, but that is a part of her she has really taken pride in. She wants to speak up. It is that we learn to be able to talk up and have rights as women, to be able to say what we believe, and then we have to go back to this world where you can't.

## "Marcia in Elementary School"

**Ma:** Being a good student in middle school, I would hide when people would ask me what was on my report card. You would have to pretend you were not smart but you really wanted to be smart and you really wanted to succeed. At the same time, you were not going to let anybody know. I got so embarrassed when I was in fourth grade and the teacher announced to the whole class, "There is one student who got 100% on her test and that was Marcia." I started crying. I cried because I was very shy and the last thing I wanted was to be noticed for being smart when smart wasn't cool. Isn't that awful?"

**Mi:** We had a student do that yesterday.

**Ma:** Exactly, and I think of how much worse it would be if it were something, I mean, okay, in school people tease smart kids, but what if it is something that is really not accepted—like Waffa and Rusha—it is not accepted by their culture to be assertive, but we are accepted for that here. It just breaks my heart.

# Author Index

# Subject Index